WOODEN SHIP

WOODE

Chief contributing photographers:
Fred Hoogervorst, Benjamin Mendlowitz, Allan Weitz

N SHIP

THE ART, HISTORY, AND REVIVAL OF WOODEN BOATBUILDING

PETER H. SPECTRE and DAVID LARKIN

Principal photography by Paul Rocheleau

Houghton Mifflin Company

Boston   London   Melbourne   1991

A David Larkin Book

We would like to thank the following for
their help and cooperation in the preparation
of this book.

Maria Anderson, Kathleen Brandes, Maynard Bray,
Fred Brooks, Peter von Busch, Arne Emil Christensen,
Birthe Clausen, Joe Garland, Liz Gwillim, Sibylla Hasum,
Llewellyn Howland III, John Hudson, Eric Kentley,
Brian Lavery, Paul Lipke, Kenneth C. Martin, Hugh Messner,
James Moore, Allen and Liz Rawl, Mike Rines, David Spence, Eric Speth,
John Valliant, Jean de Vandière, and especially
Jon Wilson
and the folks at
WoodenBoat
Brooklin, Maine

For information about permission to reproduce selections from this book,
write to Permissions, Houghton Mifflin Company, 2 Park Street, Boston,
Massachusetts 02108.

Library of Congress Cataloging-in-Publication Data

Spectre, Peter H.
    Wooden ship : the art, history, and revival of wooden boatbuilding
    / Peter H. Spectre and David Larkin.
      p.   cm.
    "A David Larkin book."
    ISBN 0-395-56692-4
    1. Ships, Wooden — History.   2. Naval architecture — History.
3. Shipbuilding — History.   I. Larkin, David.   II. Title.
    VM144.S64   1991
    623.8′207 — dc20   91-12341
                                        CIP

FCI 10 9 8 7 6 5 4 3 2 1

CONTENTS

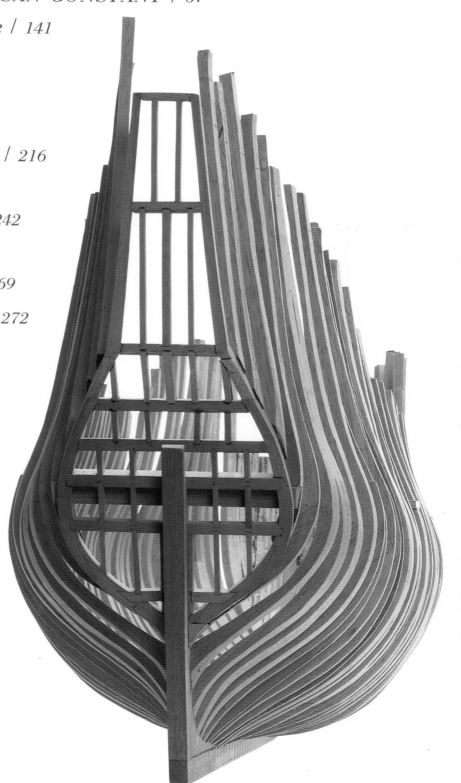

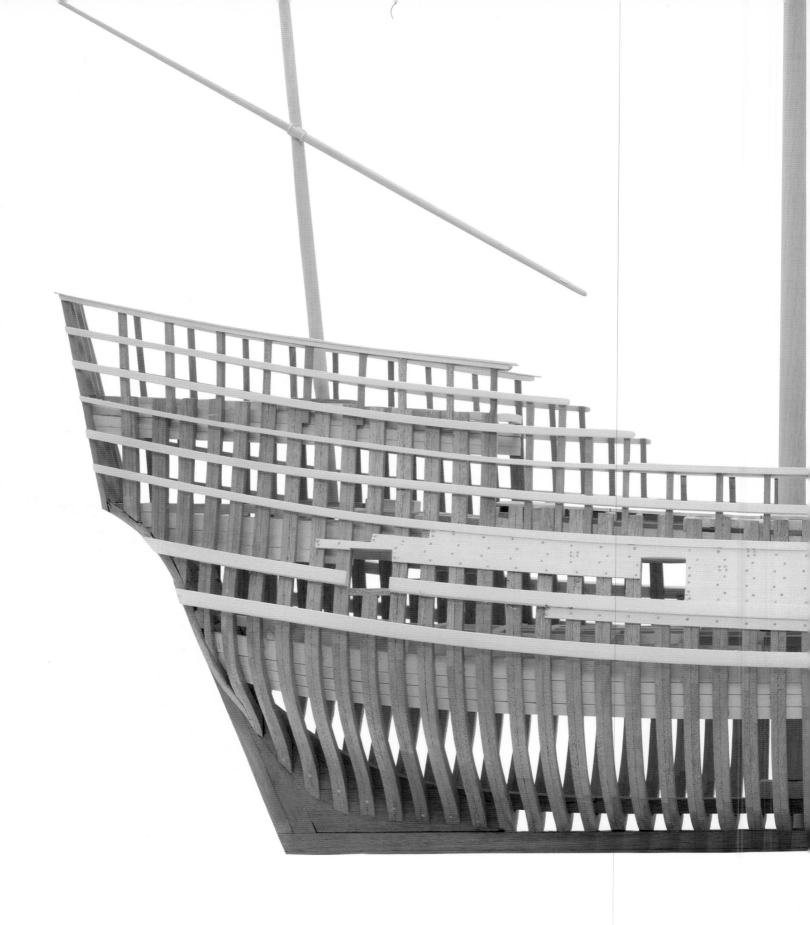

to
the Shipwrights
of the reproduced
SUSAN CONSTANT

INTRODUCTION

She was radiant, she was of an immortal beauty, that swaying, delicate clipper. Coming as she came, out of the mist into the dawn, she was like a spirit, like an intellectual presence. Her hull glowed, her rails glowed; there was colour upon the boats and tackling. She was a lofty ship (with skysails and royal staysails), and it was wonderful to watch her, blushing in the sun, swaying and curveting. She was alive with a more than mortal eye. One thought that she would speak in some strange language or break out into music which would express the sea and that great flower in the sky. She came trembling down to us, rising up high and plunging; showing the red lead below her waterline; then diving down till the smother bubbled over her hawseholes. She bowed and curveted; the light caught the skylights on the poop; she gleamed and sparkled; she shook the sea from her as she rose.

There was no man aboard of us but was filled with the beauty of that ship. . . .

The old mate limped up to me, and spat, and swore. "That's one of the beautiful sights of the world," he said. "That, and a cornfield, and a woman with her child."

— from *A Tarpaulin Muster: A Memory,*
JOHN MASEFIELD

SAILORS THINK OF A SHIP as a living creature, a symbolic body on a metaphorical journey. They say she is born on the day of her launch and dies on the day of her destruction, and during the time between is on a voyage through a genuine, vital, breathing life. In their minds, she experiences the emotions and passes through the stages typical of the human condition — the joy of creation, the passion of youth, the steadiness of middle age, the sadness of decline, the grief of death, even the glory of redemption. They say she lives like them and they like her.

On launching day, the newly built ship lies like an immobile lump on the launching ways — perhaps beautiful, perhaps not, but without life. Then the shipwrights knock her free and she slides into the water and there she is — bobbing, dipping, moving to the wind, the heaving sea, the hand of her master. She is so obviously alive that you would swear she had a soul.

Scientists and fluid dynamicists claim to know why this is so. They say that buoyancy — the upward force of a fluid on a body placed in it — creates the illusion of aliveness in a ship, so on one level all ships and boats, no matter what material they are built of — iron, steel, aluminum, fiberglass, composites — will seem alive if they are designed properly. But strangely enough, a wooden ship in the same circumstances will seem *more* alive.

The reason for this is elusive. Those with an analytical frame of mind would say that the natural buoyancy of the wood itself, beyond that caused by the shape of the hull, has much to do with this quality. Others of a more artistic bent would say that, like art, the essence would involve the eye and the sensibilities of the beholder — the smell of wood, its feel, random grain, richness, elegance.

Whatever the reason, the wooden ship has an elemental, living presence that causes sailors to speak of her as if she were a person — in particular, a female person. Even if the vessel were named after a man, as many of them are, it still would be referred to by her builders and sailors as *she*. ("I sailed aboard the *Harry L. Belden*," said the Gloucester fisherman. "*She* was the most beautiful schooner on the Grand Bank.") Such an inconsistency may seem odd to a landsman, but it is as logical to a seaman as the ebb tide following the flood. The beauty of ships; the beauty of women. One is the same as the other.

Indeed, a wooden ship has the anatomy of a living body. There is, for example, a backbone. There are, for another example, ribs. There are muscles and tendons (the rigging), and skin (the planking), and a vast number of pieces and sections named after various parts of the body — the *head, buttocks, forefoot, tail* piece, *knee, breast*hook, *eyes, cheeks, collar, knuckle, thumb* cleat, *waist,* and more.

This sounds like an elaborate construction, and it is. The wooden ship is the most complex wooden structure devised by man, a vast three-dimensional sculpture built from countless pieces of wood fit together like a jigsaw puzzle. Yet the first vessels, originating so far back in time that there are no records of their first use, are surmised to have been exceedingly simple: the raft and the dugout. (Both types, as primitive as they may seem, can still be found in use today, just because of their simplicity.)

The dugout, however, is a more complex structure than it would appear. The complexity lies in its artistry, as the builder of a dugout canoe must have the ability to imagine the shape of a boat inside the raw cylindrical shape of the felled tree. The dugout, after all, is a pure sculpture, and the dugout builder must view his work the same way his spiritual cousin, the sculptor-artist, does his: He must cut away every part of the log that is not a boat.

The art of shipbuilding has always demanded the ability to use the imagination to think in three dimensions; only relatively recently in the evolution of the wooden ship has the builder had the luxury of formal plans. For centuries, the closest thing to plans was a model, a miniature sculpture, carved before the builder began construction. In many cases, the builder didn't even use a model; rather, he depended on patterns of the ship's critical elements or a few notes or merely the mental image of what the boat should look like. It is no wonder that the builder of wooden boats and ships has always been seen as an artist as much as a craftsman. In fact, many of the early books on shipbuilding and the associated trades carried such titles as *The Art of Shipbuilding*, or *The Art of Rigging*, as if to reinforce that concept.

In the modern era, there is a distinct separation between ship design and ship construction. The designer and the builder seldom are the same person. Yet in the old days, the designer usually was the builder as well. *What* was done was interwoven with *how* it was done and the limitations of the material with which it was accomplished. The person who ordered the ship could call for a very wide and full hull for carrying capacity, with extremely fine ends for speed, but if the material would not conform to that shape, or if the builder did not have the technology to make the material conform, then the construction would not work. The sensible method, then, was for the builder to design the ship, rather than depend on someone else who might or might not understand how wood works.

The design of ships, after all, has always been influenced by the material and method of construction. Although wood is a very forgiving shipbuilding material, certain shapes can be achieved in wooden ship construction and others cannot. The experienced builder can tell at a glance whether or not a design is buildable, and, like those with an artistic sensibility, he will maintain — with no logical explanation, merely with a statement of gut feeling — that if she looks good, she will be good.

The latter declaration of aesthetics has nothing to do with the superficial decoration of a ship. Many ships have been embellished with fine art — carved figureheads, elaborately painted and gilded stern galleries, bas-relief trailboards, and the like — but no shipbuilder or designer would ever maintain that such artworks in themselves would make her a good ship. Beautiful, perhaps, but not necessarily a good sailer or a fine seaboat. No, beauty to the shipbuilder has to do with the fairness of a well-lined planking, a properly raked stem, the heart-stopping elegance of the perfect sheer, a hull so finely proportioned that the vessel would seem to glide through the waves like a greyhound at sea.

Art indeed may be a principal component of wooden ship design and construction, but it is not the only one. Craftsmanship is an absolute necessity; no matter how clearly the builder can see the shape of the vessel in his mind's eye, he cannot build the ship without both the skills and the appropriate technology for the job. Proper tools and the ability to use them are indispensable for the builders of all wooden vessels, from the primitive dugout of prehistory to the complex clipper of the nineteenth century, from the simple flat-bottomed skiff to the modern racing yacht.

Wooden ship building technology has always developed in tandem with the technology of society at large. Without the tools for felling trees and shaping wood, the devices for moving trees and lumber from the forest to the workplace, the fastenings for holding pieces of wood together, neither houses nor boats could be built. In later years, without advanced engineering knowledge — how to construct large objects of many pieces of wood held together in such a way as to handle extreme stress — huge barns, railroad trestles, ships capable of voyaging to distant seas could never have been built.

The engineering knowledge for bridge building, for example, is very much related to that required for shipbuilding. Not surprisingly, I. K. Brunel, one of the pioneer bridge and railroad builders of nineteenth-century England and the premier engineer of his age, was also a ship designer and builder. His engineering knowledge was indispensable to the construction in 1837 of the *Great Western*, the largest wooden steamship of the time.

By Brunel's era, wooden ship construction had evolved far beyond the raft and the dugout into a system whereby various pieces of timber were formed and fastened together to produce the complex shape of the hull. Long before Brunel, two basic methods had developed: (1) shell first, where the skin of the boat, the planking, was built first and interior framing added later; and (2) skeleton first, where the backbone and framing were built and then the skin was planked over it. Shell-first construction was suitable for relatively small vessels but not for large ones, so eventually it was superseded by skeleton-first construction, although the former never died out completely. (The shell-first method is still used to build some small craft, particularly in Scandinavia, Arabia, and India.)

Edge-fastened shell-first construction was the major method of Western antiquity. The Cheops ship, the world's oldest surviving wooden vessel, was of that type. A Bronze Age ceremonial ship dating from 2650 B.C., she was discovered in a chamber at the base of one of Egypt's great pyramids. (Her ancestor was the papyrus raft, reeds bundled into the rudimentary shape of a boat — a type that still exists on Lake Titicaca in the Andes of South America.)

Skeleton-first construction permitted the development of vessels suitable for large-scale exploration, commerce, and warfare. Columbus's ships were built with that method, as were all the major vessels from his era to the present — the ships that explored the East and the West, the great fleets of the Napoleonic Wars, the clipper ships, the downeasters, and the huge coasting schooners of the late nineteenth and early twentieth centuries. It is safe to say, in fact, that if skeleton-first ship construction had not been developed when it was, the pace of exploration and development would have been slower and the course of history before the era of iron and steel ships would have been considerably different.

There is a school of thought that maintains the wooden ship is dead, made obsolete by twentieth-century technology. In theory, vessels built of steel, aluminum, fiberglass, and the various composites are better. They may be cheaper, easier, and quicker to build, and, if maintained properly, they may last longer, stand up to the ravages of the sea better, and cost less to operate. But even the most avid supporters of such vessels must admit that they lack a certain undefinable essence that is inherently present in a wooden ship. Call it heart or soul; spirit, vitality, vigor, romance, or zest; the ability to arouse the senses of touch, sight, and smell. Whatever it is, wooden ships have it and the others seldom do.

The wooden ship has a rich past, a fascinating present, an all-but-inevitable future. In this book we examine these unforgettable craft, the best of the best of the best.

SIMPLE CRAFT

The dugout, despite its primitive origins, is still used in many parts of the world where tall, large-diameter trees are available. The simplest dugout is a log of suitable size that has been shaped on the outside with an axe. The inside may have been hollowed by burning away the excess wood or by cutting it out with chisels and gouges and, if the tool was available, an adze. Such a boat is limited only by the size of the log.

In the absence of large-diameter logs, more complex dugouts have been built by splitting the hollowed log down the middle and adding a filler piece to produce a wider hull, or by filling the hollowed log with hot water to soften the wood and then forcing the sides outward. To make the dugout more seaworthy and give it more carrying capacity, some builders have used the simple hollowed log as a foundation and built up the sides with planks.

Simple form, simple function. The common rowing skiff can be found around the world. A boat for all classes, it is a rough-and-ready little craft used by everyone from fishermen to yachtsmen. Other names for this plain rowboat are *flat*, *flattie*, and, because in profile it resembles an old-fashioned clothes iron, *flatiron skiff*. It is inexpensively and easily built by bending side planks around a form, fastening them to a flat transom and a sharp stem, and planking the bottom.

Both of these boats — one modern, one old — were built by craftsmen with an intuitive understanding of the way the wood's inherent characteristics suggest the shape of a hull. Not without justification, these craft personify the old boatbuilder's saying that what looks good *is* good, and elaborate decoration has nothing to do with the matter.

Scandinavian craft, and those of other regions inspired by them, come to us from the Viking era. They have changed little, either in shape or in basic construction method, from those times. Like most objects of Scandinavian origin — seagoing or landbound — they are perfect examples of the principle that form follows function.

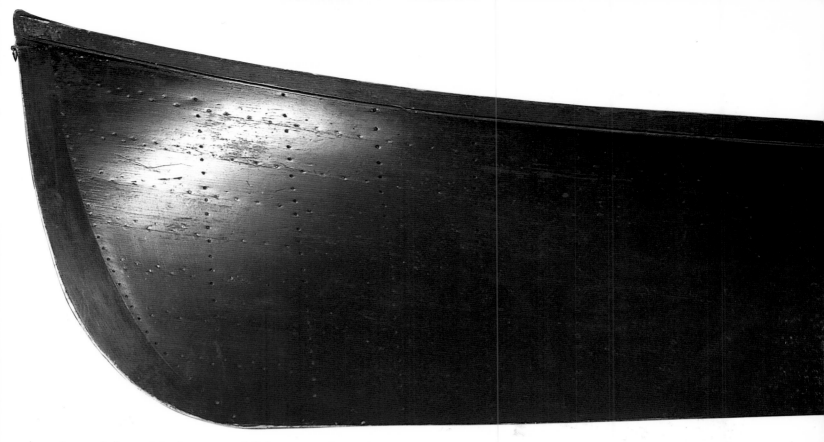

A rowing craft favored by hunters and fishermen and designed for lightness, speed, and carrying capacity, the Adirondack guideboat is living proof that much of the beauty of watercraft comes from economy of style and the craftsman's sensitivity to material. Since guideboats are carried from one lake or stream to another, they must be light enough to be lifted by one person yet strong enough to stand up to the stresses of vigorous use. Constructed with an engineer's sensibility and an artist's eye, they have extremely thin planking, delicate frames, and tiny nails.

19

Improving technology may change the construction of wooden boats, but the timelessness of good design remains. The shape of this double-paddle canoe — named for its paddle with blades on both ends of the shaft — has its origins in boats of the latter half of the nineteenth century, but it has been built with modern materials. Constructed like ancient Scandinavian craft, with the lower edge of one plank overlapping the top edge of the next (*lapstrake* in America; *clinker* in Britain), its planks nevertheless are of very thin plywood and are held in place with waterproof glue rather than metal fastenings. This little canoe is so light it can be carried over the shoulder like a book bag, yet it is significantly stronger than most boats twice its weight.

In a construction sense, this little canoe represents the most recent stage in the evolution of wooden boat construction. In the earliest times, vessels beyond the dugout were built shell first — that is, they were planked first and the frames were fitted afterward to hold the shape. Later, they were built skeleton first and then planked. Now, in a throwback to ancient times, this canoe was built shell first. The difference is that frames were not fitted afterward. The strength of the modern materials used in the hull is such that no frames are necessary to maintain the shape of the skin.

A small, round-bottomed recreational rowboat, a few inches longer than 12 feet, yet her structure is the same as that of a wooden ship ten times her size. Granted, she doesn't have the deck of a ship or the massiveness and complexity of a ship's timbers, but the lack of those elements makes the appreciation of her construction that much easier. Once again, this is engineering by an artist, the parts amalgamated into a whole that is light, strong, beautiful — each piece of wood chosen for the special characteristics dictated by its function. Cedar for light, rot-resistant planking, oak for strong frames, mahogany for contrasting color in the sheerstrake (topmost plank), and spruce for strength with lightness in the oars.

The construction of a boat like this is significantly more complicated than that of a flatiron skiff, even though both might share the same overall dimensions. The skiff would use a couple of planks for each of the sides, a dozen or so planks for the bottom, a few frames, and a handful of parts for the stem, transom, and seats. This boat, on the other hand, is constructed of hundreds of individual pieces, each shaped to fit precisely into the next like a jigsaw puzzle.

left

A purpose for everything, everything with a purpose describes this New England–style rowing boat, which has an almost Puritan simplicity, bordering on severity, to its parts. The handles of the oars are left unfinished to provide a better grip for the rower; the hard edges of the seat, floorboards, frame, and knees are softened to prevent injury; the floorboards are removable to facilitate the bailing of rainwater; gaps are left between the individual pieces of the seat to allow moisture to drain into the bilge. The hole in the seat can accommodate the mast for an auxiliary sailing rig.

above

Many of the best small wooden boats for pleasure use are adaptations of working craft. This rowing dory — as sharp as a knife, yet its major parts are only two plywood side planks, a bottom plank, a transom, and a stem — is a refinement of the old-style Grand Bank fisherman's dory. Lighter, narrower, less high-sided than its ancestor, the Gloucester light dory, as this is called, retains the seaworthiness of the Bank fisherman's dory yet has the bonus of speed under oars.

A properly designed wooden boat is not a thing alone
but an integral part of its environment. *Where* it is
used and *how* it is used are just as important as what
it is. This pulling-boat type evolved in the tidal rivers
and harbors along the coast of Maine, and it exhibits
many of the characteristics one expects to find in that
region: strength combined with fineness of form,
handsomeness acquired from tradition — an honest,
straightforward, down-home craft.

The temptation is to call this a lowly workboat, for that is what it is: a Matinicus Island peapod, originally developed for the Maine coast lobster fishery. Working-class origins or not, this is a thoroughbred, designed for seaworthiness and carrying capacity and built for strength and durability. Generically known as a double-ender — like a canoe, the bow and the stern are pointed — the peapod gets its name from its resemblance to the pod of a pea split open at the top.

Working watermen demand much from their craft, and therefore a boat used to haul lobster traps cannot be maintained like a yacht. This peapod has a workmanlike finish and nothing more. The topsides have a flattish-white paint to camouflage dings and blemishes in the hull, and the bottom has copper paint to prevent fouling by weeds and barnacles. The inside is saturated with oil — probably a mixture of linseed oil and turpentine — to protect it from rainwater and salt spray.

A study in contrasts, and graphic evidence that a wooden boat's intended use determines how it will be built.

The long, narrow craft at the left is a reproduction of a rowing racing boat from the early nineteenth century. It is lightly but strongly built, and, because "flash" contributes much to the sporting life, it is beautifully finished like a yacht. There are seats for four oarsmen, each to a single oar, and a coxswain — the steersman — in the stern.

The craft above is a waterman's skiff, used for crabbing and oystering alongshore. It is more heavily built and has the utilitarian finish favored by fishermen. There are two forward rowing stations for her crew; the after part of the boat is left free for workspace and stowage. The board with low sides extending from rail to rail is used by the watermen to cull, or sort through, their catch.

The Whitehall style of pulling boat, of which the Boston Whitehall is a variant, was developed in New York City in the 1820s and quite likely took its name from Whitehall Street, where it is thought the first examples of the type were built. Anywhere from thirteen to twenty feet long, it was used variously as a harborfront workboat, a rental boat, a water taxi, and even as a racing boat.

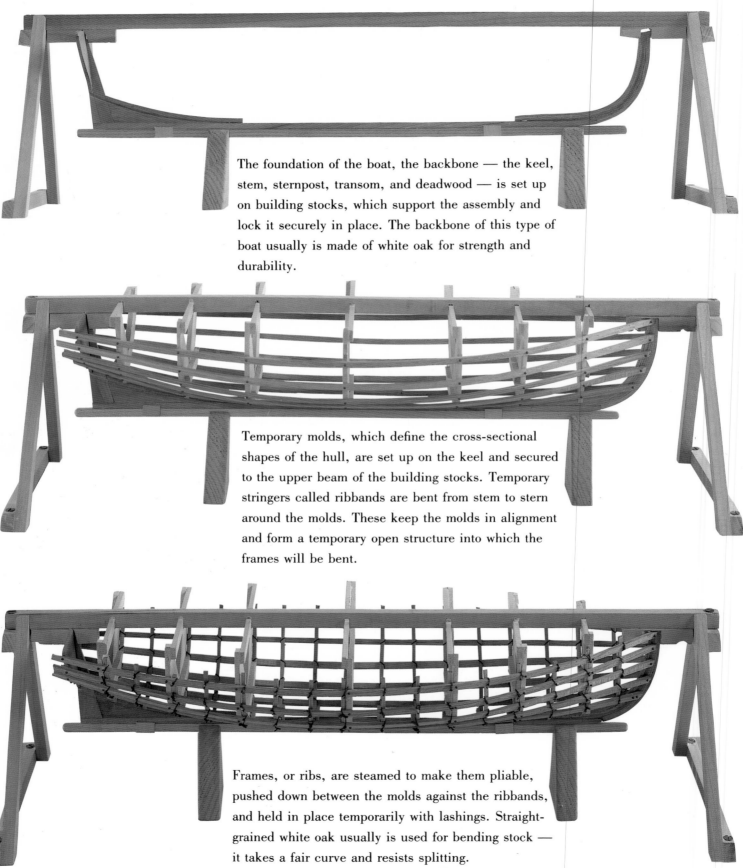

The foundation of the boat, the backbone — the keel, stem, sternpost, transom, and deadwood — is set up on building stocks, which support the assembly and lock it securely in place. The backbone of this type of boat usually is made of white oak for strength and durability.

Temporary molds, which define the cross-sectional shapes of the hull, are set up on the keel and secured to the upper beam of the building stocks. Temporary stringers called ribbands are bent from stem to stern around the molds. These keep the molds in alignment and form a temporary open structure into which the frames will be bent.

Frames, or ribs, are steamed to make them pliable, pushed down between the molds against the ribbands, and held in place temporarily with lashings. Straight-grained white oak usually is used for bending stock — it takes a fair curve and resists splitting.

The hull is planked. The ribbands are removed as the planking progresses and the planks are fastened directly to the frames. To prevent the hull from twisting out of shape, the builder alternates from one side of the boat to the other as he planks. Because the hull is fuller in the middle, each strake, or run of plank, must be tapered at the ends. Cedar typically is used to plank a boat like this, as it is light, strong, easily bent, rot-resistant, and takes finishes well.

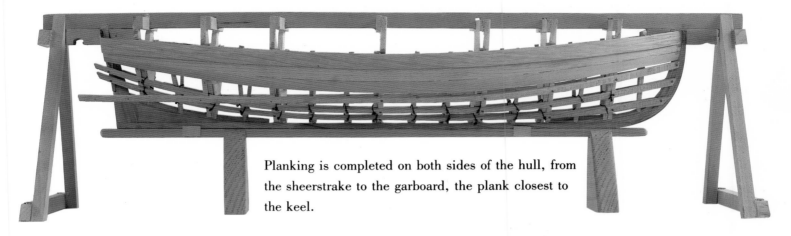

Planking is completed on both sides of the hull, from the sheerstrake to the garboard, the plank closest to the keel.

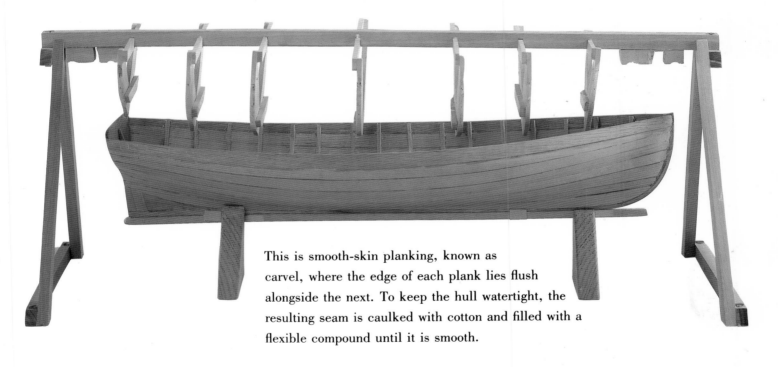

This is smooth-skin planking, known as carvel, where the edge of each plank lies flush alongside the next. To keep the hull watertight, the resulting seam is caulked with cotton and filled with a flexible compound until it is smooth.

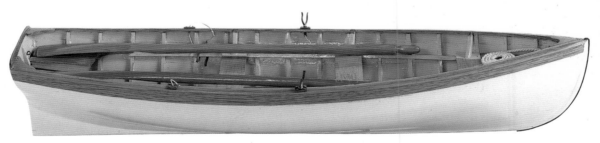

The completed boat has been finished out with rubrails, seats, oarlocks, and oars, then painted and varnished.

Bark canoes are the traditional watercraft of North American Indian tribes. Perhaps the most organic of wooden boats — using no metal fastenings and made solely of materials gathered from the forest — they have been constructed for centuries in a variety of shapes distinctive to their regions. To build them, only the simplest of tools are required: a wooden chisel to remove the bark from the tree, a froe to split the cedar planking and frames from the logs, a crooked knife for carving and fitting, and an awl to punch holes for sewing the seams.

An Indian — or a white man, for that matter — with the knowledge of the bark-canoe building art, could walk into the woods with a handful of tools and walk out with a perfectly proportioned canoe that was buoyant, resilient, and light enough to be portaged from one waterway to another. What's more, he could repair and maintain the craft as he went, using patching and waterproofing materials readily available in the forest.

This canoe built by Henri Vaillancourt of New Hampshire is of the style common to the Abenaki tribe of Maine and New Brunswick. It was constructed skin first — the inside of the bark on the outside of the canoe — from the white or paper birch tree (also known as the canoe birch). The bark was stripped from the tree in a single sheet, laid on the ground, and then folded up to form the sides of the hull. Stakes driven into the ground held the sides in place while the stems, interior planking, thwarts, ribs, and rails were fitted. The seams along the stems were sewn with thread split from spruce roots. Clamps made on the spur of the moment with odd bits of wood were used to hold the two sides together at the stem. The seams were waterproofed with a homemade sealant of rosin, grease, and linseed oil.

31

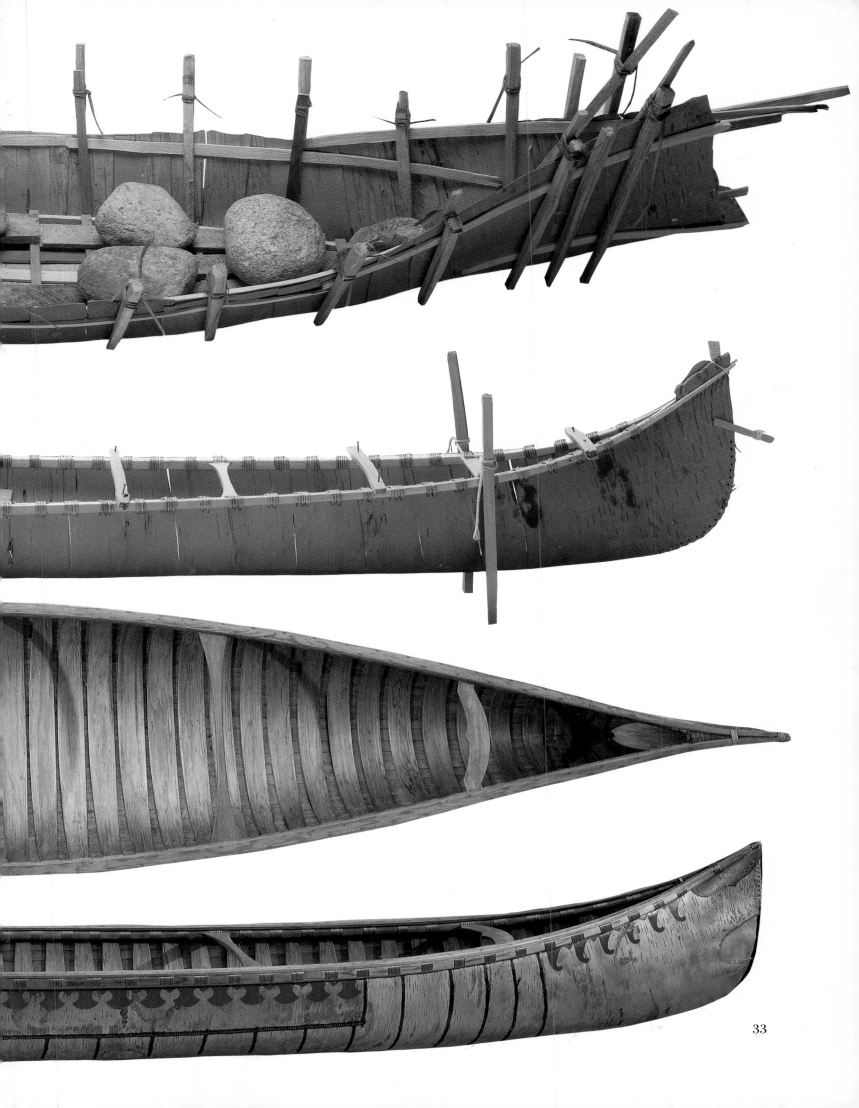

The red glare fell on the weather-beaten features of the Leather-stocking, whose tall person was seen erect in the frail vessel, wielding, with the grace of an experienced boatman, a long fishing spear, which he held by its center, first dropping one end and then the other into the water, to aid in propelling the little canoe of bark, we will not say through, but over the water.

The boat glided along the shore and moved onto the land, with a motion so graceful, and yet so rapid, that it seemed to possess the power of regulating its own progress. The water, in front of the canoe, was hardly ruffled by its passage.

Elizabeth examined the light ashen timbers and thin bark covering of the canoe, in admiration of its neat but simple execution, and with wonder, that any human being could be so daring as to trust his life in so frail a vessel. But the youth explained to her the buoyant properties of the boat, and its perfect safety, when under proper management.

— from *Leather-Stocking Tales*,
JAMES FENIMORE COOPER

An early Chesapeake five-log canoe. Note that the sides have been built up higher with sawn planks. Though this type of construction — shell first — has been practiced into the twentieth century, it dates back to ancient times.

When European explorers first reached the Chesapeake Bay, they found Indians plying the waters in dugout canoes. DeBry, in his *Grandes Voyages*, published in 1590, described how these canoes were built after a pine tree of the proper size was felled:

The tree is raised upon a platform built on forked posts at a height convenient for working. The bark is stripped off with sharp shells; the inner length of the trunk is kept for the bottom of the boat. A fire is made all along the length of the trunk, and when it has burned sufficiently it is quenched and the charred wood scraped away with shells. Then they build a new fire, burn out another piece, and so on, sometimes burning, sometimes scraping, until the boat has a good bottom.

Eventually colonists on Chesapeake Bay in Virginia and Maryland took up dugout building themselves, but they required larger craft than a single log could provide, so they learned to build boats from several pine logs pinned together — two-, three-, even five-log canoes.

For a five-log sailing canoe, the builder began with a keel log, which was roughly hewn to shape with an axe and an adze. Two more logs, known as garboard logs, were hewn to fit alongside the keel log, and then another two, the side or wing logs, were shaped to fit them. The individual logs were roughly shaped before they were permanently joined — in the early years with wooden dowels or mortise-and-tenon joints and in later years with iron drift pins. The hull then was given its final shape and fitted out with deckbeams, decking, and a sailing rig. Such was the skill of the builders that the resulting boat was difficult to distinguish from one that had been constructed of planks laid over frames.

Log canoes were used for fishing, oystering, and light cargo carrying by the watermen of the Chesapeake well into the twentieth century, but now they are used strictly for racing under sail. Some of those still under sail date from before the turn of the century.

left

Chesapeake log canoes used for racing carry a huge press of sail, too much for the hull to handle in anything more than a moderate breeze. To compensate for this, they carry planks that can be extended to windward. The sailors then become movable ballast; their weight counterbalances the hull, preventing the canoe from capsizing.

preceding page and above

The ancient Egyptians were building ships at least by 2650 B.C., the date of the Cheops ship, discovered in a tomb beneath the pyramids, though they seldom sailed out of the Nile River into the Mediterranean.

This ship, from approximately 1480 B.C., was of the type that made trading voyages to the Land of Punt, a country still unidentified by Egyptologists. Built shell first of timbers from the palm tree, an extremely flexible wood, it was suitable only for lake or river

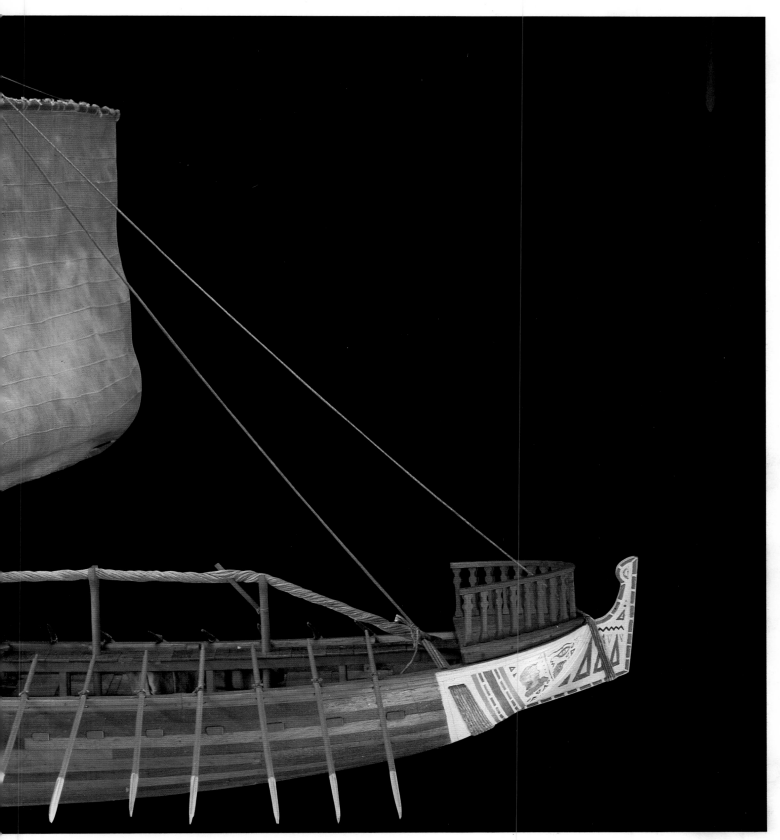

travel, as it would have been too loose and unseaworthy to stand the stresses of an open-sea voyage. As it was, the ancient ship's builder had to use a rope truss, held under tension, to keep the hull from falling apart. This truss system — shown held by posts above the ship's rail — may seem crude, but it has been used even up to recent times, when many long-hulled steamboats and ferries were fitted with similar wood or steel trusses to prevent the ends of the vessels from drooping.

By the time of Rome's ascendancy, great fleets of ships were sailing the Mediterranean, as the continued existence of the far-flung empire depended on trade and communication. The warships of the era were powered by oars for speed and maneuverability. The merchant vessels — known as round ships because of their more rounded shape, to increase carrying capacity — generally were powered by sail. This model of a Roman round ship of approximately 50 B.C. is based on the type on which St. Paul may have sailed to Malta, where he was shipwrecked in a storm.

When day broke they could not recognize the land, but they noticed a bay with a sandy beach, on which they planned, if possible, to run the ship ashore. So they slipped the anchors and let them go; at the same time they loosened the lashings of the steering-paddles, set the foresail to the wind, and let her drive to the beach. But they found themselves caught between cross-currents and ran the ship aground, so that the bow stuck fast and remained immovable, while the stern was being pounded to pieces by the breakers.

— Acts of the Apostles 27, *New English Bible*

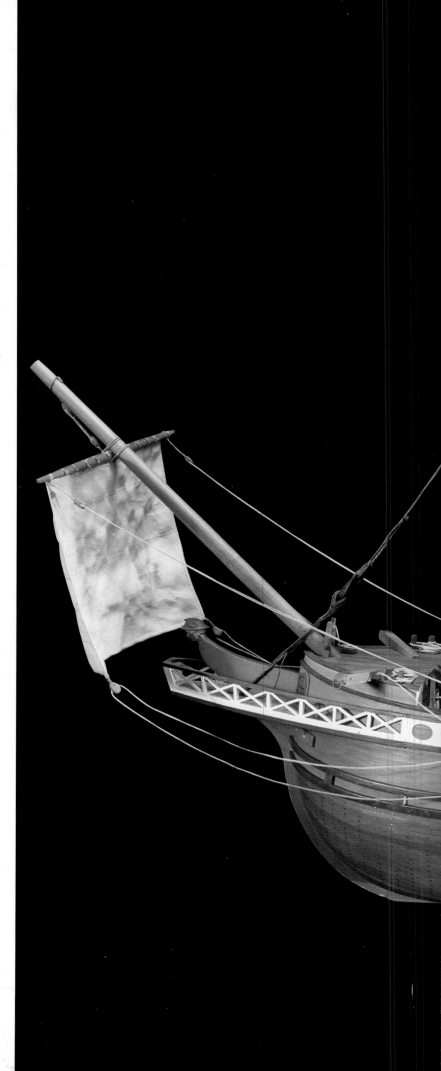

THE VIKINGS

From the fury of the Norsemen, good Lord deliver us. — medieval prayer

THEY WERE CALLED VIKINGS — sea rovers — and they swept out of Scandinavia in open ships with dragons carved on the stems and colored shields hung over the rails. For a few centuries on either side of the end of the first millennium, they slashed and burned their way up and down the coast of Europe and the British Isles, even crossing the great ocean to Iceland, Greenland, and North America. They were warriors first, settlers second, and they profoundly influenced the course of Western civilization.

The Vikings had just as great an influence on ship design and construction. Their vessels — of which the essential elements remain today in traditional Scandinavian craft — are among the most functional fighting ships ever built. Light for their length, flexibly constructed, fast, and maneuverable, they were propelled by a single squaresail for offshore work and with oars for close, inshore work.

In 1904, an ancient Viking ship was found buried in the ground on the Oseberg farm near Tønsberg, Norway. Dating to the ninth century A.D., the 70-foot vessel was a tomb for two women and contained hundreds of artifacts, including many items used in everyday Viking life. The ship itself, however, had been crushed by the weight of the earth covering it. Even though virtually all of the parts were present, putting the ship back together proved to be an arduous, time-consuming task.

Although the Oseberg ship resembles the Viking warships in shape and construction, it is smaller and was more likely a pleasure craft or a short-haul coasting vessel. Unlike other ships of the era uncovered by archaeologists, it has more carving and decorations than usual. Decoration on the fighting ships, apart from figureheads and tail carvings, usually was accomplished with color — red, purple, and gold stripes on the planking, brightly painted oar blades and warriors' shields, and colored designs on the sailcloth.

While smooth-skin construction, in which the edges of the planking lie flush against each other, was a southern European tradition, the Scandinavians, going back to the Viking era, favored lapstrake or clinker construction. This involves a style of planking where the top edge of one plank is overlapped by and fastened to the bottom edge of the next, producing an effect like clapboarding on a house. The whole structure is reinforced with frames fitted to the inside of the hull. Lapstrake construction produces a light, strong, flexible hull, with seams (if the planks are fitted properly) that require little or no caulking to make them waterproof.

A reproduction of the Oseberg ship is eased along from its building site to the launching ramp. Because of their relatively light construction and the lack of additional weight from decks and deck structures, Viking ships were easily launched and retrieved, freeing the sailors from the constraints of fixed bases for provisioning and repairs. The Vikings were, in effect, guerrillas of the sea.

Several years were required to rebuild the Oseberg ship to its original state. Approximately 90 percent of the vessel contains original timber; only those pieces that were crushed too badly were replaced. The ship is now on permanent display with two other ships, several boats, and hundreds of artifacts at the Viking Ship Museum in Oslo, Norway.

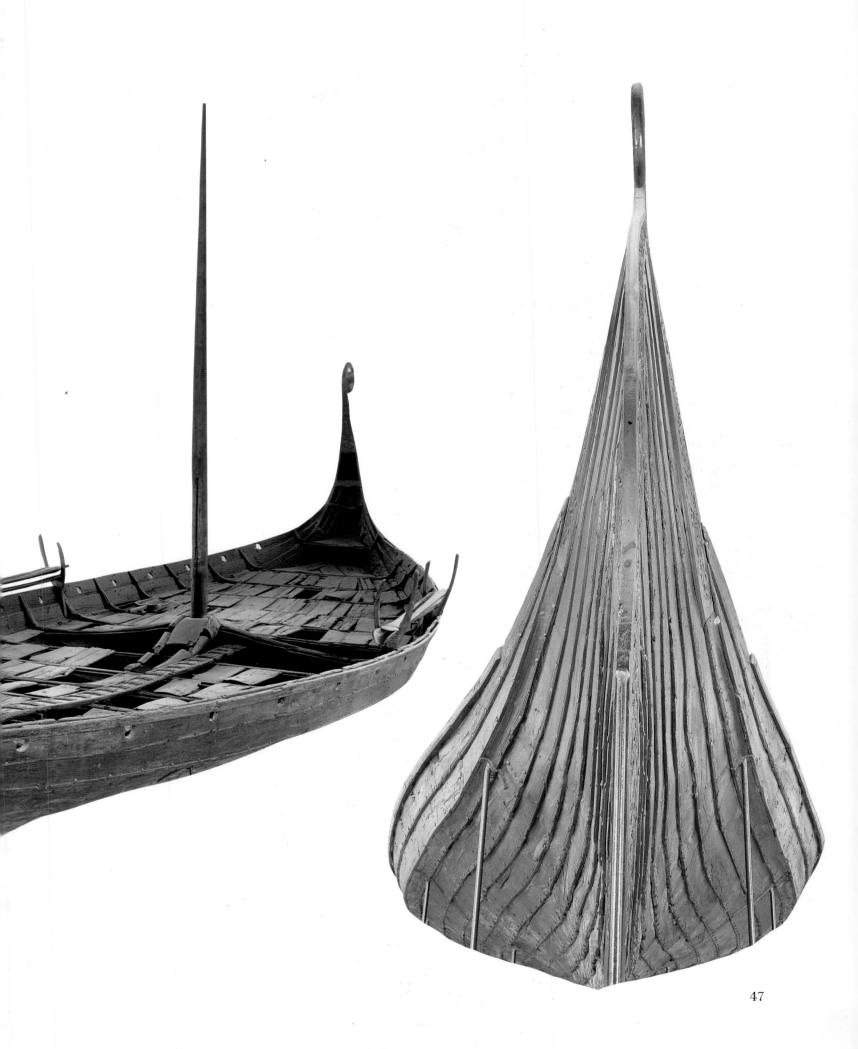

47

The Gokstad ship, also an ancient tomb, was discovered buried on a farm near Sandefjord, Norway, in 1880. Dating to the tenth century A.D., a century younger than the Oseberg ship, at 76 feet long it is also larger. Nevertheless, it is similar in function to the Oseberg ship — a coastal vessel, known as a *karv*, for inshore sailing — not a longship used by the sea rovers. It, too, was found with hundreds of artifacts, including three small boats in excellent condition.

Like her sister in the Viking Ship Museum, the Gokstad ship is almost totally original, with only a small percentage of new wood to replace pieces that were missing or too badly damaged. Unfortunately, the tops of the stem and sternpost were not found, so conjectural pieces, without decoration, have been added. She is still a remarkable example of the art of shipbuilding as practiced by the Norsemen a thousand years ago. How seaworthy was the Gokstad ship? A replica of her, built in 1893, sailed across the Atlantic to America in twenty-eight days.

A replica of a Viking ship sails over the underwater site, outlined with white buoys, where her predecessor was excavated in Roskilde Fjord, Denmark. There have been several Viking ship finds over the years, but few can surpass the spectacular Roskilde discovery, as the site contained five everyday working vessels, not elaborate burial tombs, providing a more realistic view of early Scandinavian seafaring. Lying in shallow water in the fjord were the partial remains of two warships, two trading ships, and a fishing vessel, all dating to approximately a thousand years ago.

It is thought that the ships in Roskilde Fjord were sunk intentionally to create a blockade and thus prevent marauding sea rovers from using a deeper channel in the shallow fjord to reach a village that otherwise would have been unprotected from seaward. At the time of their sinking, they were old, used-up vessels. Archaeologists retrieved the wrecks by building a waterproof wall around the site and pumping out the seawater.

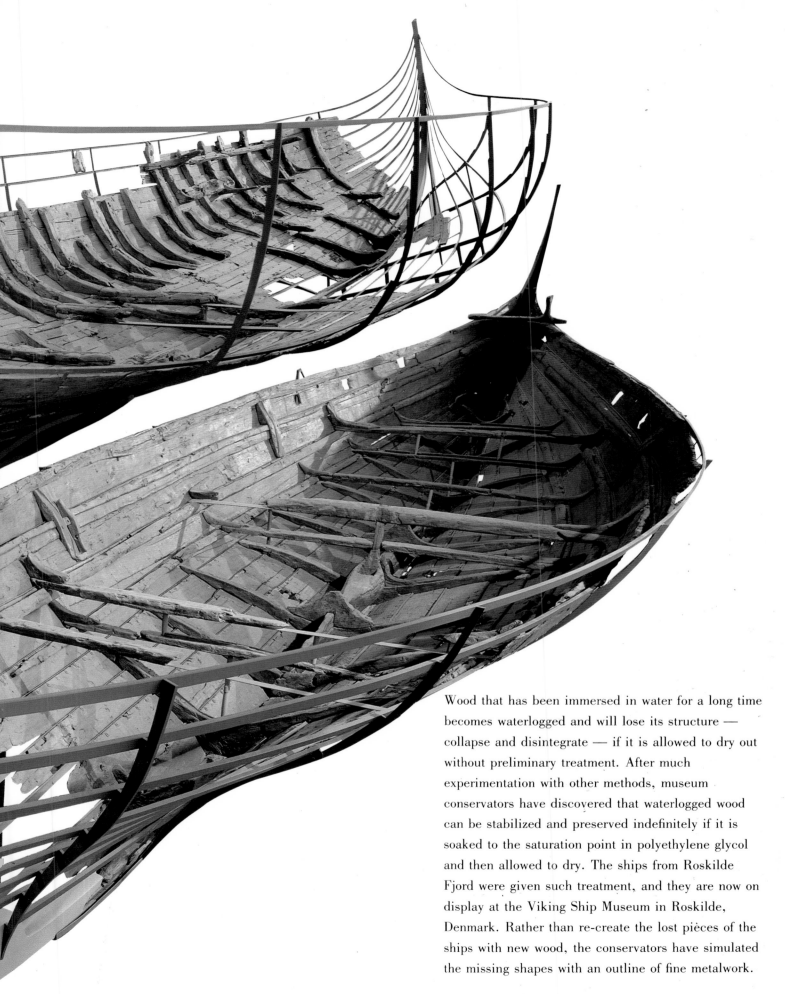

Wood that has been immersed in water for a long time becomes waterlogged and will lose its structure — collapse and disintegrate — if it is allowed to dry out without preliminary treatment. After much experimentation with other methods, museum conservators have discovered that waterlogged wood can be stabilized and preserved indefinitely if it is soaked to the saturation point in polyethylene glycol and then allowed to dry. The ships from Roskilde Fjord were given such treatment, and they are now on display at the Viking Ship Museum in Roskilde, Denmark. Rather than re-create the lost pieces of the ships with new wood, the conservators have simulated the missing shapes with an outline of fine metalwork.

To gain a better understanding of Viking-era shipbuilding methods, and also to see how such ships perform under sail, the Roskilde museum built a replica of one of the ships found in the fjord. An authentic re-creation, it was built with age-old tools and materials, right out in the open, fair weather and foul, next to the sea. This is shell-first construction in its unadorned form, a straightforward method of building a ship without complicated jigs and molds.

The hull was built right side up. The stem and sternpost were preshaped to receive the ends of the planks and then fastened to the keel, which was shaped and set on posts in the ground. The backbone assembly was braced to keep it from shifting and planking began from the keel. Each plank was shaped to ensure the curvature of the bottom and the sides, and lapped at the top edge by the next plank. As the planking progressed outward and up, shores were placed to retain the shape of the hull.

Stones were placed in the hull to splay the planking outward. The shoring on the outside and the stones on the inside helped retain the shape of the hull before the frames were fitted. Note the long pole extending between the inside faces of the stem and sternpost, and the bracing used to keep those members plumb.

Frames cut from specially selected timbers that grew roughly in the proper shape — crooked wood — were fitted to the inside of the hull. This required endless cutting and trimming for the frames to fit exactly to the changing shape of the skin. Here, the shipwrights are fastening a longitudinal member that will support athwartship (side-to-side) beams. Their wooden clamps are of an ancient, simple, but very effective design.

The finished vessel is now rigged for rowing and sailing along the Danish coast. The only modern materials here are the crew's sleeping bags and foam mattresses. Note the steering board, or rudder, fixed to the right-hand side of the stern. The Vikings always hung the steering board on this side — the steering-board side, or steerboard — a term that comes down to us as the starboard, right-hand, side of a ship as seen when facing forward. (The left-hand side is known as the port side.)

57

The Normans, Norsemen, were descended from the Vikings. Even though no one has found remains of the ships used by William the Conqueror, the Norman king who successfully invaded England in A.D. 1066, scholars believe they were similar to the longships of the Vikings. The evidence is in the famed eleventh-century Bayeux Tapestry, which shows double-ended lapstrake-planked ships propelled by oars and a squaresail set on a single mast. William's invasion ships, then, would have been larger versions of the Oseberg and Gokstad ships. This model of such a vessel is based on pictorial evidence from the tapestry and physical evidence of the Gokstad ship.

The methods for building traditional Scandinavian wooden craft have changed little since the Viking era. Even their shapes remain much the same. Here, a small double-ended rowing boat is underway. The builder has set up the backbone assembly — consisting of the keel, the stem, and the sternpost, all of which has been beveled to accept the planking. He is now fitting the garboard strake, which is the run of plank closest to the keel.

In this type of construction, the shapes of the strakes and their angle to the keel determines the final shape of the boat. There are no plans for this. The builder is, in effect, designing the boat as he goes along, based on acquired knowledge, a "feel" for what is right, passed down through the generations.

The builder has fit and fastened the garboards on both sides of the hull and is working on the next pair of strakes. Each strake is made of a couple of shorter planks fastened together with a scarf joint, in which the ends are cut at an angle to a feather edge and then joined. Rather than using stones to splay the garboards to the correct angle in relation to the keel, this builder uses posts wedged down from the ceiling of the shop.

The builder uses homemade clothespin-style wooden clamps, in company with wedges, to hold the planks in position before he fastens them permanently. The ends of the planking are fastened to the stem or the sternpost, and the overlapping edges — this is lapstrake, or clinker, construction — are fastened to each other. After the entire shell of the hull has been finished, the builder will then cut, fit, and fasten interior frames to help maintain the shape of the boat.

OCEAN SAILERS

THE MARITIME ACHIEVEMENTS of the Vikings were considerable — especially their successes in voyaging to Iceland, Greenland, and North America — but their ships were not suitable for major long-distance exploration and the large-scale transportation of trade goods. The Age of Exploration, beginning with the navigations of the Portuguese and Spanish in the fifteenth century, required larger, stouter ships. Columbus's vision impelled him to cross the Atlantic to the New World; his ships actually carried him there.

Few ships have provoked more scholarly interest than the *Santa Maria*, the flagship of Christopher Columbus's squadron of 1492, yet tangible evidence of what she looked like is virtually nonexistent. There are no contemporary plans of her; no drawings, sketches, or models. The best evidence is oblique references to her in a résumé of Columbus's journal (the original was lost).

The fifteenth century was a pivotal period in the development of the wooden ship. The smaller, open vessels — propelled as much by oar as by sail and primarily built shell first, like the Egyptian, Roman, and Viking ships — gave way to the larger, decked sailing ships that were seaworthy and robust enough to make extended open-sea voyages. To modern eyes, the *Santa Maria*, which was approximately 78 feet long by 26 feet wide, may seem small and insignificant, but her accomplishments, and those of later vessels of her era, are proof enough of her capabilities.

Columbus was not fond of his flagship. He thought her draft (depth of hull) was too great, and that she was "not suited for voyages of discovery." He also noted later in his career that "the ship I took with me on my first voyage was cumbersome."

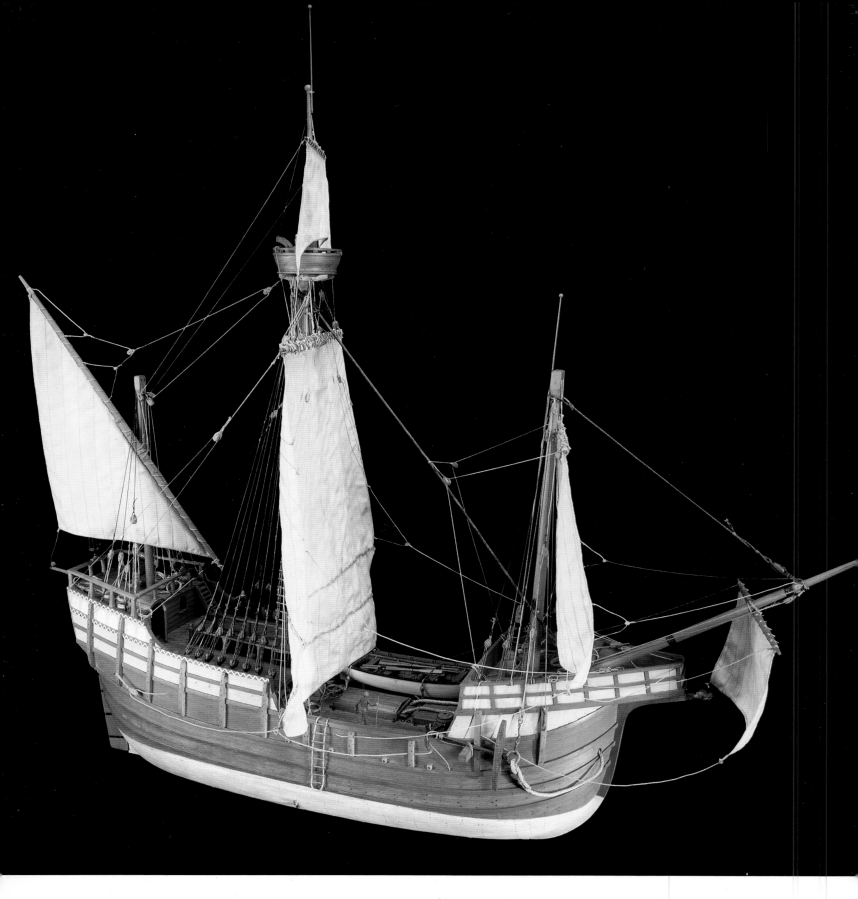

Columbus referred to the *Santa Maria* as *la nao*, the ship. Scholars have assumed she was a carrack, and most modelers and naval architects have depicted her as such — wide, deep, high-ended, fitted with three masts and several sails. In construction, the *Santa* *Maria* was the polar opposite of the Viking ships. She was built skeleton first, as were all the ships of the great voyages of discovery following the Vikings, and she was carvel planked; that is, her planks were laid edge-to-edge to provide a smooth skin.

Without any surviving evidence of Columbus's ships, we must look elsewhere to find a ship of the approximate era (fifty years later, in fact). The Solent, a body of water off Portsmouth, England, is the venue.

One of the most famous shipwrecks of the sixteenth century was King Henry VIII's *Mary Rose*, which sank in the Solent on July 19, 1545. One of England's first modern sailing battleships and the pride of the Royal Navy, the *Mary Rose* was maneuvering in calm winds off Southsea Castle, preparing to join the rest of the English fleet in battle against a much larger French force. A sudden gust of wind heeled the vessel over, immersing a row of open gunports that were just above the waterline. Within seconds, the ship began to founder. In less than a minute, according to one

horrified eyewitness, she sank with "one long wailing cry." There were some seven hundred men aboard; thirty survived. Thousands of people on the Southsea shore, including King Henry himself, had assembled to watch the great battle between the English and French fleets, and all witnessed the disaster. The subsequent British naval victory on that day was forever overshadowed by the sudden sinking, stunning in its quickness — almost as if the *Mary Rose* had been sucked down by some unseen force.

Several attempts were made to salvage the *Mary Rose* shortly after she sank, but none were successful. The centuries passed; eventually the exact location of her bones was forgotten. Then, in 1971, a team of underwater archaeologists, searching the bottom of the Solent for historic shipwrecks, discovered the remains of the vessel; almost half of her, the starboard side, was preserved in the mud of the sea bottom. A little more than a decade later, the *Mary Rose* was raised and taken to a special conservation chamber in Portsmouth, where she is today on display.

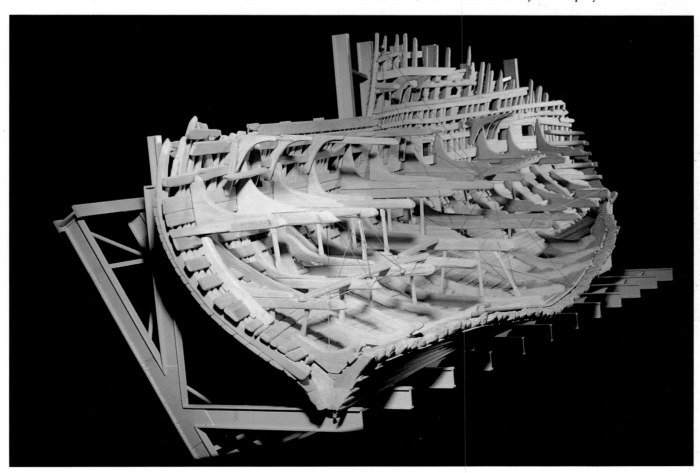

Even though less than 50 percent of the *Mary Rose* survived after more than four centuries on the sea bottom, enough of her exists to provide historians with an unparalleled view of the construction of a Tudor-era warship, particularly the structural members required to handle the weight of her heavy cannons. In contrast to the relatively lightly constructed Viking ships of a few centuries earlier, the wooden warships of the Tudors and later generations were true engineering marvels, complicated vessels that demanded immense amounts of materials and a vast shipyard establishment to build and maintain them.

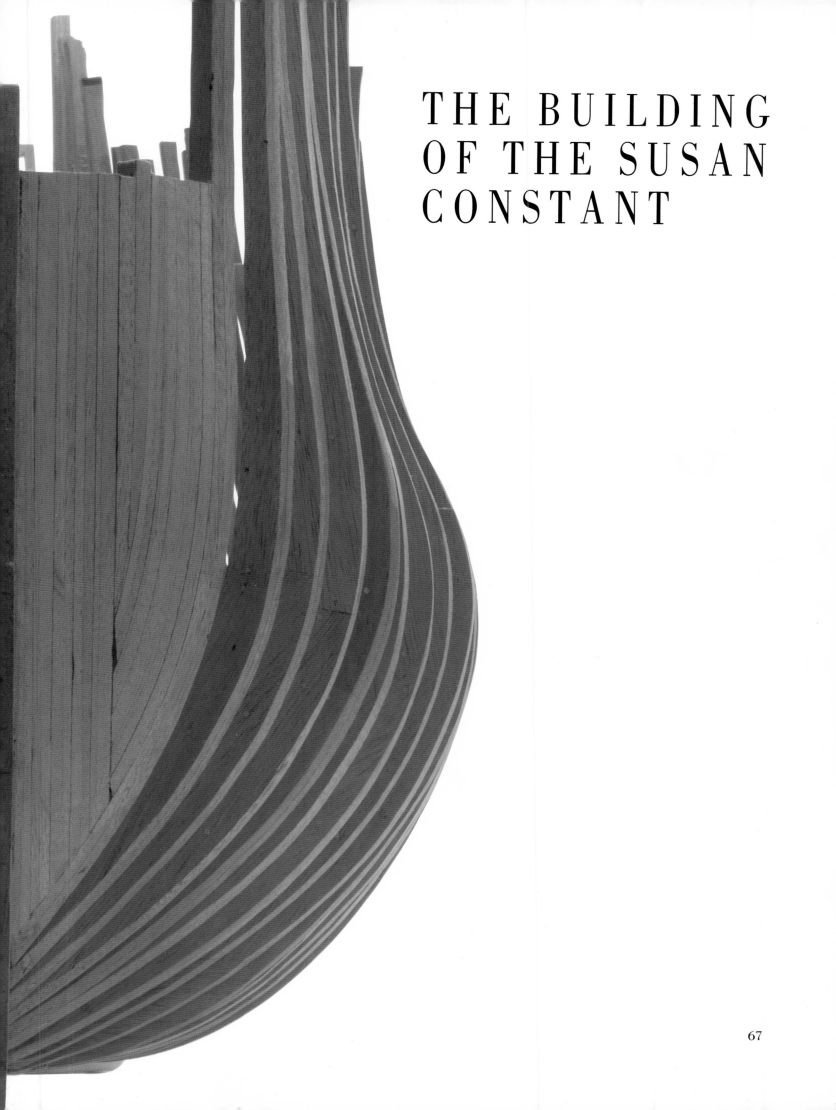

THE BUILDING
OF THE SUSAN
CONSTANT

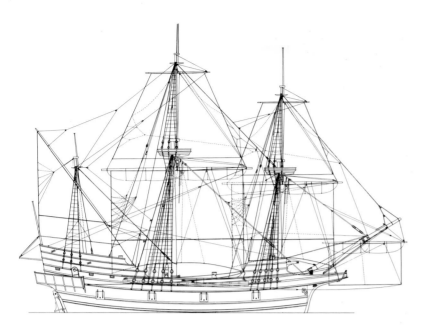

LATE IN THE AFTERNOON of April 26, 1607, three tiny
vessels entered Chesapeake Bay from the Atlantic Ocean and
came to anchor under Old Point Comfort on the peninsula formed
by the James and York rivers. They were the *Susan Constant*, the
Godspeed, and the *Discovery*, chartered by the Virginia Company,
127 days out of London, England, by way of the Canary Islands
and the Caribbean. They were under the overall command of
Captain Christopher Newport, after whom Newport News was
named, and carried 144 passengers and crew, among them the
celebrated captains Bartholomew Gosnold and John Smith. The
expedition's mission was to establish a settlement on a river of
their choice that tended inland in a northwesterly direction, as
European explorers still believed that the east coast of America
was connected to the west coast by a northwest passage through
the heart of the continent.

Within weeks, a colony was established at Jamestown, near the
mouth of the James River; it would become the first successful
permanent English colony in North America, preceding the
Plymouth Colony by thirteen years.

The *Susan Constant*, the flagship of the expedition, was a typical
small merchant trading vessel of the era. Little is known about
her before the Jamestown voyage, but historians believe she was
most likely built in a shipyard on the River Thames about a year
before she set sail from London. All that is certain about her
physical dimensions is that she was 120 tons; naval architects,
comparing this figure with data for other, better-known vessels of
her type, surmise that she must have had a keel length of 55
feet, width of 23 feet, and 9½-foot depth of hold.

To modern eyes, the *Susan Constant* appears top-heavy and clunky, almost primitive when compared to the mighty clipper ships of two and a half centuries later. But her design was the result of careful consideration. Here is what Sir Henry Mainwaring wrote in *The Seaman's Dictionary* about proper ship design of that period:

The bow is of great importance for this first breaks the sea and is that part which bears all the ship forward on when she is pressed down with sail, which is in a manner the bearing of the ship. If the bow be too broad the ship will not pass easily through the sea but carry a great deal of dead water before her; if it be too lean or thin, she will pitch or beat mightily into a hollow sea for want of breadth to bear her up, so that there must be a discreet mean betwixt both these. The shaping of this part doth much import the ship's going by a wind; yet I have seen both sorts go well by a wind, but most commonly those have good bold bows; nevertheless it is certain that a ship's way after on — which is called her run — is of more importance for her sailing by a wind. The run is of main importance for the ship's sailing, for if the water come not swiftly to the rudder she will never steer well, and it is a general observation that a ship that doth not steer well will not sail well, and then she cannot keep a good wind, for if a ship hath not fresh way through the sea she must needs fall to leeward with the sea. We say a ship hath a good run when it is long and cometh off handsomely by degrees, and a bad run when it is short and that the ship is too full below.

The *Susan Constant* must have followed the above principles well enough, because she made the passage from England to Virginia and back again, despite encountering several fierce storms, and then continued on with a successful career as a general merchant trader in European waters.

A reproduction of the *Susan Constant* was built in 1956 for the 350th anniversary celebration of the establishment of the Jamestown Colony. With the reproductions of the *Godspeed* and *Discovery*, she was moored at the Jamestown Settlement in Virginia, where she was seen by thousands of visitors over the years.

Time took its toll on the little ship, however, and by the late 1980s, the *Susan Constant* was due for a total rebuild. In the intervening years, there had been significant advances in historical research and, especially, underwater archaeology, and the curators felt historical accuracy would be better served by building a brand-new ship. Brian Lavery, a British expert on wooden ships of this period, was commissioned by the Jamestown Settlement to research a new design for the *Susan Constant* based on the most up-to-date knowledge of vessels of her type. Stanley Potter, naval architect, drew up the building plans. Allen Rawl, a wooden shipbuilder from Maryland who had worked on several other historical reproductions, was engaged to build the new ship. A crew of experienced shipwrights was put together, a shop was erected, building stocks were set up, and the keel of the vessel was laid in December 1989 at the Settlement on the banks of the James River. For more than a year, visitors to the park were treated to the sights and sounds of an unfolding drama within sight of the original Jamestown Colony — the building of a wooden ship.

> *Build me straight, O worthy Master!*
> *Stanch and strong, a goodly vessel,*
> *That shall laugh at all disaster,*
> *And with wave and whirlwind wrestle!**

*This and all poetry in this section is from "The Building of the Ship," 1849, by HENRY WADSWORTH LONGFELLOW

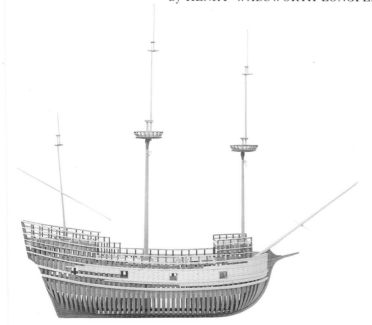

And first with nicest skill and art,
Perfect and finished in every part,
A little model, the Master wrought,
Which should be to the larger plan
What the child is to the man,

Its counterpart in miniature;
That with a hand more swift and sure
The greater labor might be brought
To answer to his inward thought.

Until a century or so ago, ships and boats were not designed on paper as they are now. The designer, who usually was also the builder, would consult with the future owner to determine the requirements of the vessel — its use, its size, the accommodations for the crew, the stowage capacity, and so forth. The designer would then carve a scale half model of the hull from a solid block of wood, or from a block made of several layers of wood pinned together, incorporating into it those shapes he knew from experience would produce the required characteristics: long and lean for speed, wide and deep for cargo-carrying ability, whatever the owner desired. This model would be of only half the hull — hence the term *builder's half hull model* — on the assumption that a hull cut in half longitudinally would be shaped the same, a mirror image, on both sides.

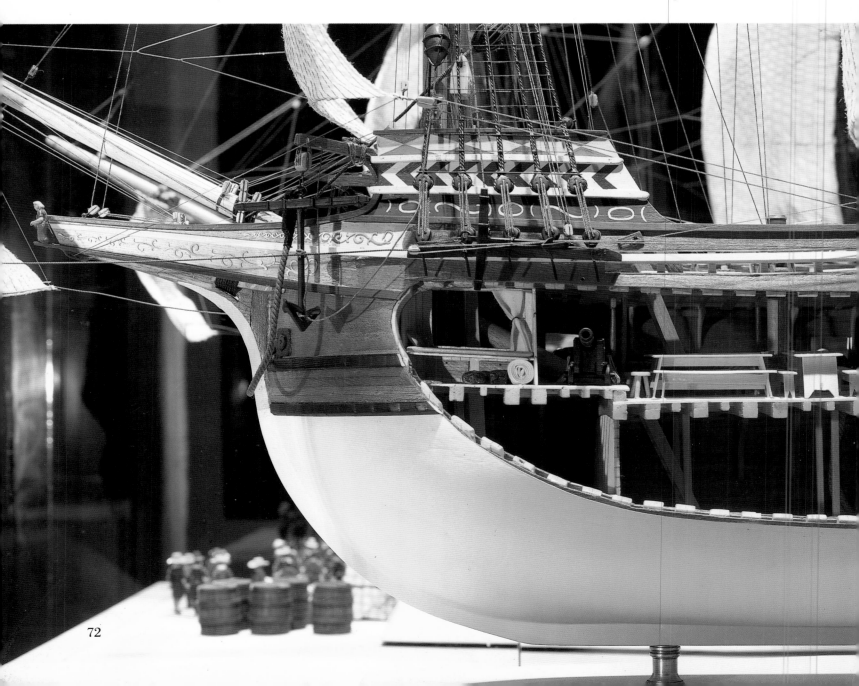

Once the designer was satisfied with the shape, and the owner concurred, the builder would take the lines of the hull off the half hull model, using various measuring devices, and draw them full size on a lofting floor — a flat, open space with a smooth surface. From these lines, which delineated in two dimensions the three-dimensional form of the hull, he would make patterns of thin wood for the principal parts: the stem, the stern, the individual frames, and so on. He would then use the patterns for drawing out the shapes of the parts on the rough timbers.

The half hull model, a working tool, was seldom used for decoration. For display purposes — perhaps as a centerpiece in the shipowner's office or home, or as a sales tool to convince wealthy backers to invest in the construction of a ship — the owner sometimes had a more elaborate model built, rigged as the vessel would be when finished. Today, in the absence of the vessels themselves, fully rigged models are built to show the details of ships of the past. Here we have a very elaborate model of the *Susan Constant*, cut away along the side to reveal the interior of the vessel.

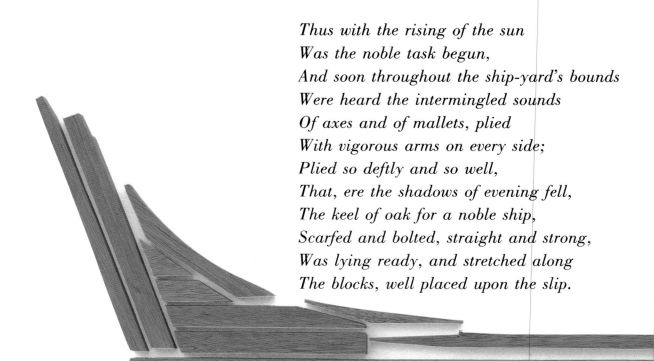

Thus with the rising of the sun
Was the noble task begun,
And soon throughout the ship-yard's bounds
Were heard the intermingled sounds
Of axes and of mallets, plied
With vigorous arms on every side;
Plied so deftly and so well,
That, ere the shadows of evening fell,
The keel of oak for a noble ship,
Scarfed and bolted, straight and strong,
Was lying ready, and stretched along
The blocks, well placed upon the slip.

Wooden hulls are subjected to several types of strains produced by such forces as the action of the sea, the effects of propulsion, and the weight of the vessel. Some of these strains are longitudinal, some transverse, and others are localized.

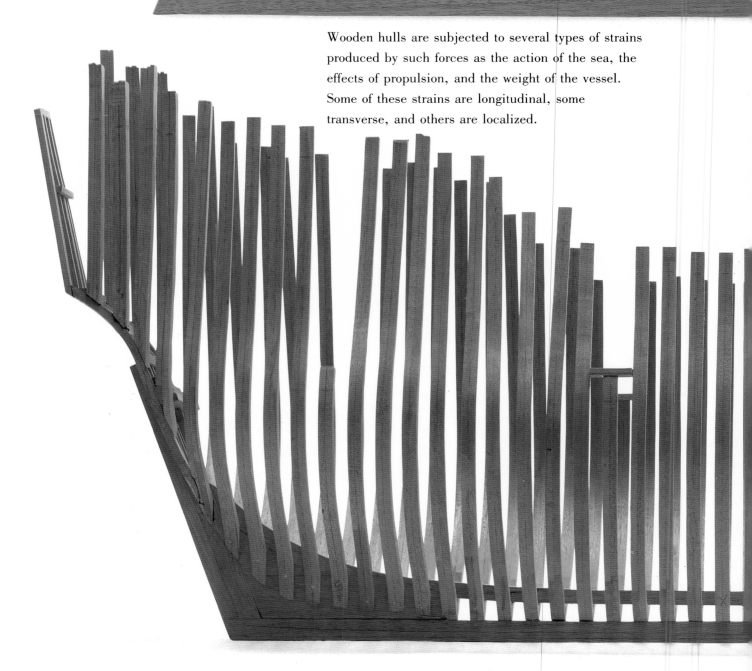

The backbone is the foundation of the vessel. Its shape determines the profile of the hull, and its structure provides considerable resistance to longitudinal and localized strains. In addition, it assists the frames and other members in resisting transverse strains. The backbone consists of three sections — the stem, the sternpost, and the keel — each made of several individual parts fastened together. The keel of the *Susan Constant* is greenheart, a tropical hardwood, noted for its strength, density, and resistance to rot.

Once the backbone has been assembled, it is set up on the building stocks, aligned, and braced.

The hull of the *Susan Constant* is a complex shape, wide in the middle and narrowing toward the ends, so a cross section of the hull at any given point along her length will be different from any other. The frames, which in effect represent cross sections, are therefore all unique in shape.

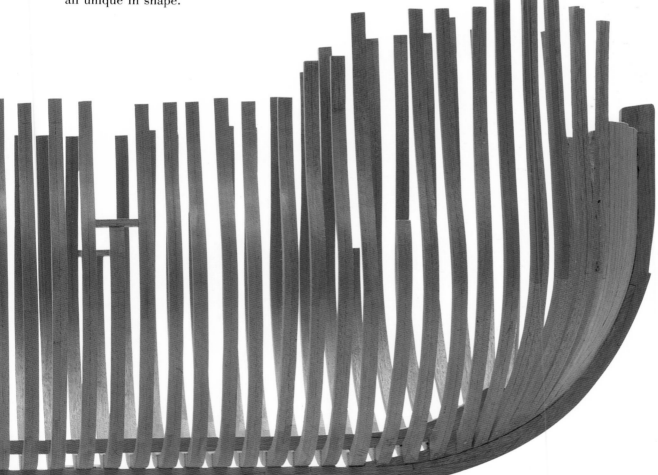

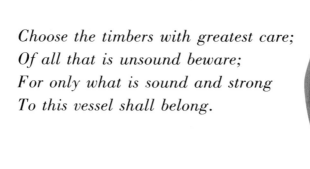

Choose the timbers with greatest care;
Of all that is unsound beware;
For only what is sound and strong
To this vessel shall belong.

Each frame is built separately, to its own complex pattern, of several pieces of wood — the *Susan Constant*'s are of such tropical hardwoods as mora, purpleheart, and courbaril — cut to shape according to patterns determined by the master builder. All of these pieces need to be curved to a greater or lesser extent, so they are sawn from crooked wood with sweeping grain. The frame maker matches the sweep of the curve to the sweep of the grain, producing a timber that retains the natural strength of the tree from which it came.

This is what is known as double-sawn construction — each frame made in two layers, each section with its own name. There are floor timbers (the lower section of the frame that crosses the keel), futtocks, and top timbers, the topmost parts of the frame on each side. The individual pieces of the frame are cut according to the master builder's pattern, beveled on the edges to follow the run of the planking, and then assembled into the whole on a framing platform specially built for the task. Hundreds of individual pieces are used to construct the vast number of frames in the *Susan Constant*, and each piece must be systematically numbered and checked.

Tar is spread between the pieces of the frame to prevent moisture from seeping into the seams and causing rot, and they are fastened together with trunnels.

left

Although metal fastenings are used throughout the ship, wooden trunnels — "treenails," thick dowels — are used as well. A hole is drilled through the members to be joined with an auger, a tight-fitting trunnel is driven with a maul to fasten the pieces together, and the head of the trunnel is sawn off. Hardwood wedges are then driven into the ends of the trunnel to lock it securely in the hole. A properly driven trunnel is every bit as effective as a metal fastening — in some cases, more so.

right

The first frame has been erected, and the shipwrights are fitting temporary braces to prevent it from shifting. Earlier, the frame-making crew nailed temporary crosspieces, known as cross spalls, to the frame to keep it from spreading at the top. This view is from the after end of the backbone, looking forward. The darker-colored wood marks the backbone and frame; the lighter wood is that of the bracing.

The frame was hauled upright by a pair of sheerlegs — a simple, crude, cranelike structure built on site by the yard crew. A block-and-tackle arrangement attached to the sternpost holds the sheerlegs upright. Another block-and-tackle attached to the forward side of the sheerlegs was used to pull the frame upright, its bottom resting on the keel. This is an ancient method for raising large, heavy timbers — surprisingly easy due to its carefully worked-out mechanical advantage.

The frames are erected, one after another, as quickly as they are constructed on the framing platform. The position of each frame is checked carefully, as any misalignment could result in crookedness or unfairness in the hull. Once the shipwrights are satisfied that everything is as it should be, they nail temporary cleats, short pieces of wood, to the inside and outside edges of the frames to keep them from shifting in relation to each other and to the keel. Side braces, or shores, are added to keep the framework from tilting to one side or the other.

The *Susan Constant*'s frames are closely spaced, but,
because she is primarily a merchant vessel, not nearly
as closely spaced as were those of wooden warships.
The latter were heavily constructed, with massive
frames and very little space between them — on the
largest, the most powerful vessels, there was virtually
no space at all — both to handle the weight of their
armament and to act as a defense against the force of
the enemy's cannonballs.

above

Whole frames are used along most of the length of the hull, but in the after section, in the vicinity of the deadwood, they must be erected in halves because of the extreme depth of the deadwood. The deadwood is in effect a huge knee that reinforces the sternpost, the vertical member at the after end of the keel that supports the stern structure and the rudder. The deadwood is built up from several individual pieces of timber pinned together and fastened both to the keel and to the sternpost.

left

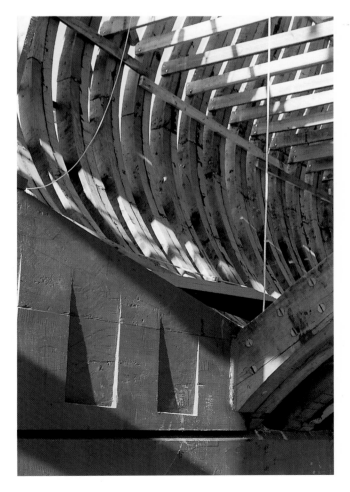

Using mallets and chisels, the shipwrights hew shallow mortises (sockets) in the sides of the deadwood to take the heels of the half frames, which must be cut to a precise angle so they align properly with the backbone. The half frames are erected in matching pairs — one on one side of the hull, its mirror image on the other side.

The backbone has been painted with red primer to protect the wood from drying too much during construction and developing checks, or cracks.

85

The skeleton of the ship emerges. The full frames of the midbody of the hull have been set up, and the yard crew has begun to work on the stern framing (the view here is from forward, looking aft). The two curved timbers on either side of the sternpost are the fashion timbers, which define the edge of the counter, or stern, of the vessel. They will be spanned by the transom timbers, crosswise members that further support the counter.

Before the half frames can be erected, they must be dragged aft along the keel: The framing platform is at the forward end of the construction ways. This may not be a full frame, but it still is quite heavy, weighing several hundred pounds. Here, two shipwrights are using a block-and-tackle to make the job easier. Note the extreme bevel at the heel of the frame, where it will be fit into its corresponding socket cut into the deadwood.

The framing of the after end of the vessel has been completed. The heel of each of the half frames has been set in the heel sockets and fastened to the deadwood with metal spikes. The heads of the fastenings have been driven below the surface of the frames so they won't interfere with the planking.

right

The stem, like the backbone at the stern, is built of several members bolted together, with tar in the joints. Painted with red primer to prevent the wood from checking, it has been braced securely to keep it from shifting.

Day by day the vessel grew,
With timbers fashioned strong and true,
Stemson and keelson and steerson-knee,
Till, framed with perfect symmetry,
A skeleton ship rose up to view!

As at the stern, the frames at the bow are erected in halves. The foremost pairs are known as cant frames, because they are not erected square to the keel like the midbody frames but, due to the shape of the bow, canted forward.

left

Visible here are the heads of the bolts that fasten together the various pieces of the stem. The temporary cleats nailed to the inside of the stem are used as steps by the shipwrights. The short vertical timbers between the cant frames and the stem are fillers known as hawsepieces.

And around the bows and along the side
The heavy hammers and mallets plied,
Till after many a week, at length,
Wonderful for form and strength,
Sublime in its enormous bulk,
Loomed aloft the shadowy hulk!

The frames hold the shape of the hull, but to add to
the strength of the whole, they must be tied together
with permanent members running the length of the
vessel and complementing the work of the keel.
Several of these longitudinals are fastened to the inside
of the hull. Their importance cannot be overestimated.
Without them, the hull, over time, is likely to sag in
the middle or droop at the ends. (The latter condition
is known as hogging.)

Another longitudinal member, the keelson, is laid over
the frames, along the top of the keel, in effect creating
a complementary interior keel. Long fastenings are
driven through the keelson and the frames, down into
the main keel, tying together all three structures.
Long, thick timbers, or stringers, are bent in from
stem to stern between the keel and the tops of the
frames, and clamped securely. They are then fastened
down with long metal spikes.

The stringers fastened to the interiors of the frames
serve triple duty: They tie the frames together, provide
significant longitudinal strength to the hull, and serve
as shelves to support the ends of the deckbeams. (The
topmost stringer, the one on which the beam end
actually rests, is called the clamp.) With the frames,
stringers, and deckbeams locked together with metal
fastenings, the basic interior framework of the hull is
completed.

The *Susan Constant*'s deck framing not only provides a firm foundation for the deck planking, which will be laid longitudinally, but also adds strength to the entire structure of the vessel. The crosswise timbers, those running from side to side, are the deckbeams. They have camber — that is, they are curved so water can drain over the side. The short timbers between the deckbeams, running fore-and-aft, are carlins. The hewn timbers up in the bow, fastened to the stem, the cant frames, and the hawsepieces, are the breasthooks. They tie the deck framing to the stem while reinforcing the bow framing. The four holes on either side of the stem below the deck framing are hawseholes for the anchor cable.

Framers and plankers are not the only craftsmen working on the *Susan Constant*. In addition, there are the sailmakers, sparmakers, riggers, carvers, shipsmiths, and others.

above

The tools of the modern sailmaker differ little from those of centuries ago: special needles, triangular in cross section, with sharp edges to cut easily into the heavy sailcloth; leather sailmaker's palms, specially shaped to the user's hand, for pushing the needle into the cloth; fids and marlinspikes — long, pointed tools — of various sizes for working rope; punches for making grommet holes; seam rubbers for smoothing out the seams; and more. Today the long seaming is done with sewing machines, but the rest of the work is still done by hand.

The *Susan Constant* will set six individual sails — one on the mizzenmast, two each on the mainmast and foremast, and one on the bowsprit — for a total sail area of slightly more than 3,900 square feet. Here, a sailmaker is sewing a boltrope to a sail to reinforce the edge. In the past, canvas was of cotton or flax. Today, the *Susan Constant*'s sails are of Duradon, a synthetic fiber that looks and feels like traditional canvas but is stronger and lasts longer.

As a common workaday merchant vessel, the original *Susan Constant* was plainly decorated, though she no doubt had a carving here and there as appropriate. Here, two craftsmen work on the catheads, timbers projecting from either side of the bow; they are used to raise the anchors clear of the bow when the ship gets under way.

right

The rigging of sailing vessels requires a vast number of blocks and deadeyes. Blocks, which consist of a wooden shell holding a pulley that revolves around a pin, are used in various combinations with rope to improve mechanical advantage. Deadeyes, on the other hand, are blocks without a pulley, thick discs of wood with holes drilled in them. (They are, in effect, dead blocks with eyes — hence the name *deadeye*.) Lanyards, pieces of line, are run through the eyes for setting up the standing rigging. Here, a blockmaker is shaping a deadeye.

The planking of the hull is a long, tedious process. It is relatively straightforward at the after section of the hull and along the midsection, but quite difficult in the bows (where the planks take a tight curve) and near the keel (where they must bend and twist at the same time). Planks that have to take sharp bends must be steamed in a steam box to make them pliable.

The master builder and boss planker begin the process by lining out the planking, determining the exact location of each strake or line of plank, and marking the widths. Although a finished hull may look as if it has been planked with straight-edged strakes of uniform width, such is not the case. Rather, the strakes vary in width to accommodate the varying fullness of the hull along its length. The proper dimensions are laid out on the rough planking stock and sawed to shape.

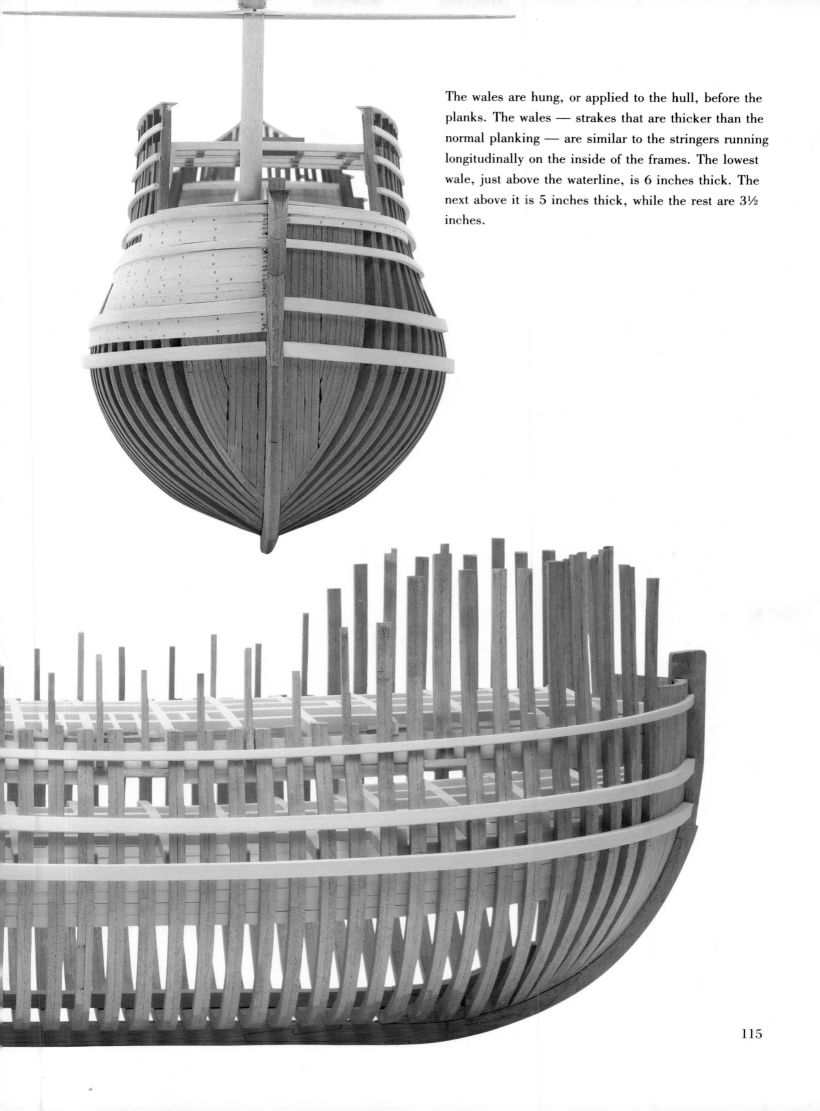

The wales are hung, or applied to the hull, before the planks. The wales — strakes that are thicker than the normal planking — are similar to the stringers running longitudinally on the inside of the frames. The lowest wale, just above the waterline, is 6 inches thick. The next above it is 5 inches thick, while the rest are 3½ inches.

115

So, too, the planking itself varies in thickness. The bottom planking is 2 inches thick; the topmost, 1½ inches. To provide longitudinal strength where it is needed — in the region just above the waterline — the planking between the lower wale and the second wale is a full 3 inches thick. The hull from the keel to the waterline is planked with courbaril, a tropical hardwood. Juniper, a softer wood from the middle Atlantic states, is used above the waterline. The planks are fastened to the frames either with trunnels or spikes or both.

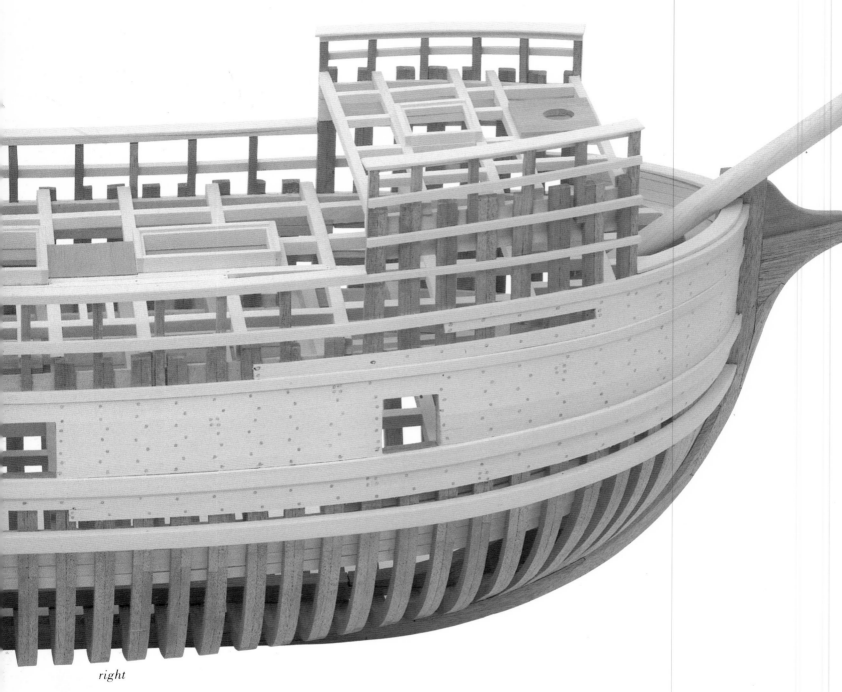

right

The hull planking is almost finished. The shipwrights have prepared to plank the main deck by fitting the waterways — thicker planks at the outside margin of the deck. The waterways are notched and beveled to fit around the projecting top timbers of the frames, which here serve as framing for the bulwarks, the high rail above the deck.

The square opening in the side of the hull is a gunport, which will be fitted later with a lid. Note the bevel along the top edge of the thick red channel wale and the black main wales below the gunport. This is not a matter of decoration. Rather, the bevel allows water to drain off the top of the wales and not become trapped in a corner to cause rot.

118

Behold at last,
Each tall and tapering mast
Is swung into its place;
Shrouds and stays
Holding it firm and fast!

The three masts of the *Susan Constant* began as trees, giant Douglas firs, in the forest. Carefully selected for their clear, straight grain, they were hewn to the proper diameter and taper in the age-old manner.

To make a mast, the shipwrights first squared the tree along its length in cross section, then tapered it — the mast is thicker in diameter at the bottom than it is at the top — then made it eight-sided, then sixteen-sided, and finally round. As can be imagined, mastmaking requires the eye of an artist and the hand of a craftsman. What's more, it produces an incredible amount of wood shavings and chips.

Once the mast itself has been made, it must be fitted with the accessories that assist in its work. The crossed timbers at the head of this mast are known as the crosstrees and trestletrees; they provide the foundation for the top, a platform for the lookout, and a miniature deck in the sky for the sailors when they work in the rigging. The rectangular piece at the top of the mast is the cap; the round hole in it holds the topmast — a lighter, higher mast that carries the topsail.

The rigging looped around the mast just above the crosstrees and the trestletrees is the standing rigging — shrouds and stays used to support the mast. Shrouds support the mast in a side-to-side direction; stays perform the same function in a fore-and-aft direction.

120

The running rigging, yet to be fitted, generally is
lighter than the standing rigging and is used for
raising, lowering, and adjusting the sails, as well as
for bracing the yards — the long, tapering spars that
cross the masts and from which the sails are set.

The seams between the planks are made watertight with caulking, strands of oakum, usually treated with oils as a preservative. Here, the ends of caulking strands have been left hanging to indicate where the caulkers have left off work for the day.

By design, the edges of the planks are not square; rather, they are planed to a slight bevel before being hung, so that two planks, edge-to-edge, will form a V-shaped seam — the back of the seam tight, the front open. The caulkers fill the seam with long strands of rolled oakum, driving it down firmly with a caulking iron — a chisel-shaped tool — that is struck with a heavy mallet. The seam is then covered with a flexible compound, putty, to smooth the surface and hold the caulking in place.

right

The work of the caulker looks simple, but it is a difficult trade to practice, since swinging the mallet, especially in tight spaces near the keel, is wearing on the body. It also requires the right touch: Too much oakum will force the seams apart; too little will produce a leaky seam. The right amount, driven perfectly, not only will keep the water out but also will contribute to the strength of the hull.

123

The captain's cabin, yet to be finished, is a study of the massive structure of a wooden ship. Thick vertical knees, called hanging knees, support the quarterdeck framing. Equally heavy horizontal knees, called lodging knees, brace the ends of the deckbeams to the side of the hull. All are bolted securely. The open doors lead to the stern gallery, an outside balcony around the after part of the ship. Much still remains to be done to the interior of the hull in the way of accommodations and storage compartments.

The planking of the lower deck has yet to be laid, but the framing has been completed. Eventually, the joiners — finish carpenters — will build in bunks and other accommodations. The *Susan Constant*, as a lowly merchant ship, was lightly armed, but she nevertheless carried eight guns, all of which were on this deck, sharing space with the crew and passengers.

above

Extra reinforcement is a fact of life on a wooden ship. The pillars help the hanging knees at the side to carry the load of the main deck. Special timbers called partners reinforce the main deck, above, where it is pierced by the mast.

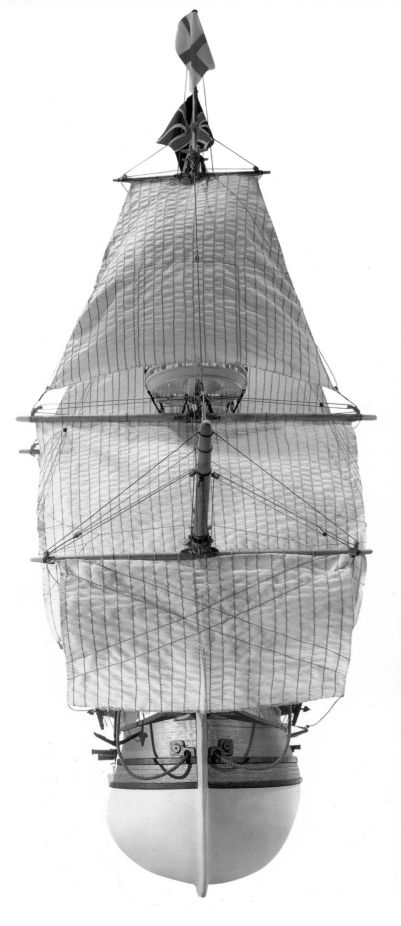

The bottom of a wooden ship must be protected from fouling by sea grass and barnacles and also from boring teredos (shipworms), which in short order can ruin planking the way termites can destroy a house.

Seventeenth-century shipwrights did the best they could, given the knowledge and technology of the time, but their techniques were nowhere nearly as effective as modern methods. A common treatment was to coat

the bottom with tar and animal hair, then sheathe it with a half- to one-inch layer of thin planking, and coat that with a white-colored mixture of oil, rosin, and brimstone — a treatment that was not very effective against warm-water shipworms. For this reproduction of the *Susan Constant*, the shipwrights used modern bottom paint, dark red in color from the presence of copper in the mixture.

127

After the hull is closed in, the decks are laid, and the masts are raised comes an incredible amount of detail work. Hardware and fastenings for a ship like the *Susan Constant*, for example, cannot be bought off the shelf; they must be handmade by the shipsmith, a blacksmith who specializes in ship fittings. The steering gear must be made and installed, the stern gallery must be constructed, the interior accommodations must be fitted, and, of course, the hull must be painted.

Considerable research went into determining authentic paint colors and designs for the hull of the *Susan Constant*. Clues were found in paintings of period ships, manuscript illustrations, and an English model of a similar ship, dating from about 1630.

With oaken brace and copper band,
Lay the rudder on the sand,
That, like a thought, should have control
Over the movement of the whole;
And near it the anchor, whose giant hand
Would reach down and grapple with the land,
And immovable and fast
Hold the great ship against the bellowing blast!

On launching day, the only evidence that this is a reproduction, not the original seventeenth-century vessel, is the presence of copper bottom paint and two bronze propellers. The new *Susan Constant* has been fitted with twin engines to increase her range and assist in maneuvering.

Then the Master,
With a gesture of command,
Waved his hand;
And at the word,
Loud and sudden there was heard,
All around them and below,
The sound of hammers, blow on blow,
Knocking away the shores and spurs.
And see! she stirs!

She starts, — she moves, — she seems to feel
The thrill of life along her keel,
And, spurning with her foot the ground,
With one exulting, joyous bound,
She leaps into the ocean's arms.

The *Susan Constant* waits at
her mooring in Jamestown, ready
for her sea trials.

The maiden voyage.

COLONIZATION
AND TRADE

Wherever profit leads us,
To every sea and shore,
For love of gain
The wide world's harbors we explore.
— VONDEL, Dutch poet

THE SEVENTEENTH CENTURY was an age of expanding trade and colonization involving most of the European nations to a greater or lesser extent. Countries with long traditions of seafaring were at the leading edge, most especially the English and the Dutch, who had competing interests in North America and the East Indies. In North America there were the Virginia Company and other commercial enterprises from England, and the Dutch West India Company from the Netherlands. In the Far East there were the Honourable East India Company, the celebrated John Company of England, founded in 1600; and the Verenigde Oostindische Compagnie, the Dutch East India Company of 1602.

The English, fresh from their defeat of the Spanish Armada in 1588, claimed the sovereignty of the seas, but the Dutch, until their final naval defeat at the end of the third Anglo-Dutch War (1672–74), could make the same claim. In 1664, for example, the Dutch were thought to have had roughly a thousand warships of various types.

The greatest of the Dutch merchant ships were the *Oostindievaarder*, the East Indiamen, the largest, stoutest wooden sailing ships of the fleet. They were designed and built for long-distance passagemaking, cargo carrying, exploration, and, most important, self-defense. They were, after all, destined for the wilds of Sumatra, Java, Borneo, the Celebes, and the Spice Islands even farther to the east.

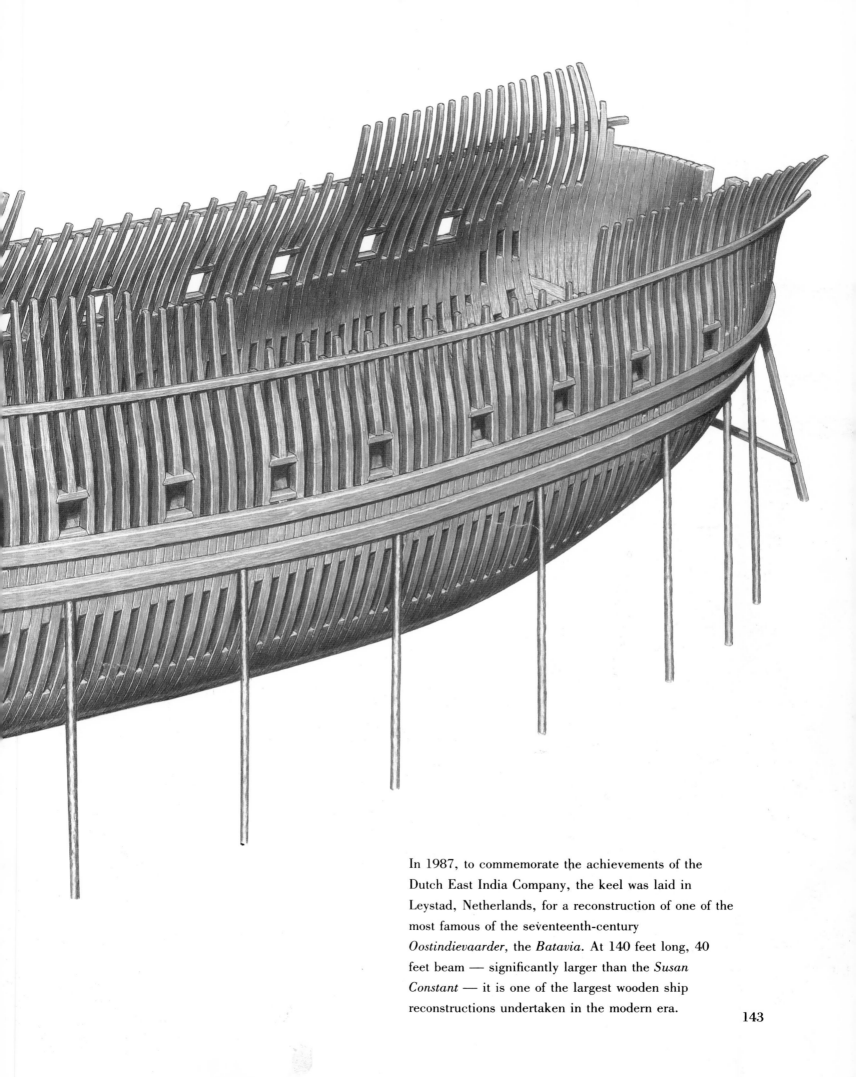

In 1987, to commemorate the achievements of the Dutch East India Company, the keel was laid in Leystad, Netherlands, for a reconstruction of one of the most famous of the seventeenth-century *Oostindievaarder*, the *Batavia*. At 140 feet long, 40 feet beam — significantly larger than the *Susan Constant* — it is one of the largest wooden ship reconstructions undertaken in the modern era.

The construction of the *Batavia* is similar to that of the *Susan Constant*. Like all major European ships from about the fifteenth century onward, the hull is built skeleton first — sawn frames on a heavy backbone, with carvel, or smooth-skin, planking. The difference, however, is in the massiveness of the construction: many more frames of significantly larger dimensions, thicker planking, thousands more fastenings, and more awkward and arduous working conditions for the shipwrights.

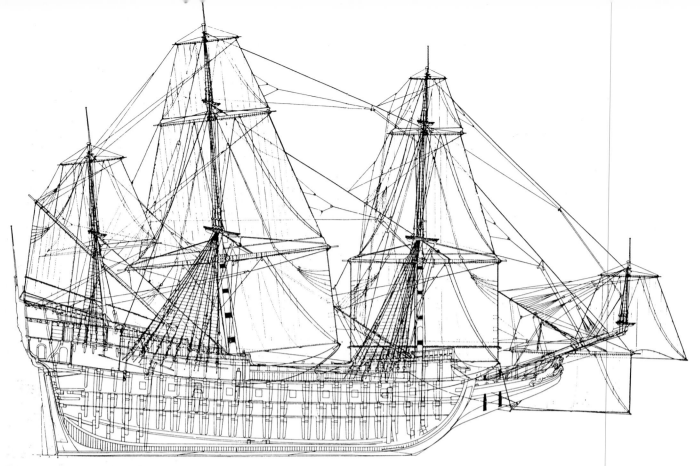

The sailing rig of the *Batavia* is only slightly more complex than that of the *Susan Constant*, but, as with the hull, it is much larger. It has taller masts of greater diameter, requiring larger timbers and heavier rigging. Although some of the elements are distinctively Dutch, such as the design of the mast caps, the method of building the masts and spars is the same. A huge, straight-grained log is made square, then eight-sided, then sixteen-sided, then round; the trestletrees, crosstrees, mast top, and cap are fitted; and the masts are stepped — that is, hoisted into place with a crane, the heel of the mast set into the mast step, a slot built over the keel.

In the interests of authenticity, the rope for the *Batavia*'s rigging, miles of it, was made in an old-style ropewalk by spinning fiber yarns into strands, which were in turn twisted into rope. A ropewalk, also known as a ropehouse, is a long shed open down the middle. Three-stranded rope, for example, is made by attaching three strands of the necessary diameter to a twisting machine, which is pulled down the ropewalk, creating a length of finished rope as long as the building. In the past, production ropewalks — those making rope for the largest sailing ships — were as long as 1,300 feet.

The original *Batavia*, built in 1627, met a tragic end. She sailed from Amsterdam in October 1628, the flagship of a Dutch East India Company fleet bound for her namesake port, Batavia, on the island of Java (now known as Jakarta, Indonesia). In her cargo of trading goods were twelve chests of silver coins and a selection of jewels — perhaps too great a temptation for some of her crew. Mutineers seized the vessel off the Cape of Good Hope; their intent was to continue on to the Far East and prey on the Dutch East India empire. But it was not to be. On June 3, 1629, the mutineers erred in their navigation and ran the ship aground on a reef off East Wallabi Island, the Abrolhos archipelago, Australia, where she broke up and sank. Most of the crew, mutineers and loyalists alike, reached shore. A few months later, a rescue ship sent out from Batavia picked up the surviving loyalists and punished the mutineers; some were marooned in Australia and the rest were hanged.

In 1963, scuba divers in search of the *Batavia*'s treasure located the vessel's remains in three fathoms of water, buried in a coral reef. They found bronze cannons, anchors, and a few coins, but not much else of value. They did, however, discover major parts of the frame and planking of the ship, among the few archaeological remains of the great Dutch East Indiamen.

The design of the modern reconstruction of the *Batavia* is based on data obtained from the wreck of the original vessel, plus contemporary plans, models, and descriptions of the Dutch East Indiamen.

Not surprisingly, given the strength of their maritime tradition, the Dutch are credited with originating the modern sport of yachting, sailing for pleasure rather than war or commerce. (The word *yacht* comes from the Dutch *jaght*, which means "hunt" or "chase.") The first Dutch yachts were shallow-draft craft suited to the thin waters of the Netherlands. Like this single-masted vessel of the mid-seventeenth century, they were based on naval vessels and working craft of the coasts, fitted out with comfortable accommodations and decorated with elaborate carvings and giltwork.

The big, fanlike board alongside the rail is a leeboard, which is lowered into the water to provide resistance to keep the shallow boat from being pushed sideways by the wind. In shoal water, the leeboard is raised to provide underwater clearance.

October 1st 1661. I had sailed this morning with his Majesty in one of the yachts or pleasure boats, being very excellent sailing vessels. It was on a wager between his other new pleasure boat, built frigate-like, and one of the Duke of York's; the wager one hundred pounds sterling, the race from Greenwich to Gravesend and back. The King lost in the going, the wind being contrary, but saved stakes in returning.

— the first recorded yacht race, from the diary of
John Evelyn

Yachting arrived in England in 1660, when the directors of the Dutch East India Company, in a gesture of friendship, presented King Charles II with the royal yacht *Mary*. The *Mary* was a miniature warship carrying a handful of cannon and a crew of thirty, and she was handsomely decorated in the Dutch style. Although early yachts were constructed heavily like warships and workboats, over time they would evolve into the comparatively lightly built vessels of today.

above and following page

In the fifteenth, sixteenth, and seventeenth centuries, European warships, especially those in the Mediterranean, were either sailing vessels or oar-powered galleys. The galleys, which were more maneuverable than sailing ships, were excellent fighting ships; witness their success in the Battle of Lepanto and their use by both sides in the critical struggle over the Spanish Armada of 1588.

The galleass was a hybrid developed near the end of the galley era — depending on one's point of view, an oar-powered ship with auxiliary sail or a sailing ship with auxiliary oars. Like all hybrids, they were a compromise — not quite as fast and maneuverable as a galley, and, because they had to carry such a large crew, without the self-sufficiency and endurance of a sailing ship. This Venetian galleass of the mid-seventeenth century was propelled with forty-eight oars, each rowed with four oarsmen. She had a lateen rig, the distinguishing characteristic being triangular sails spread aloft by long, tapering spars. She also has a spectacular amount of ornamentation on her after quarters and stern.

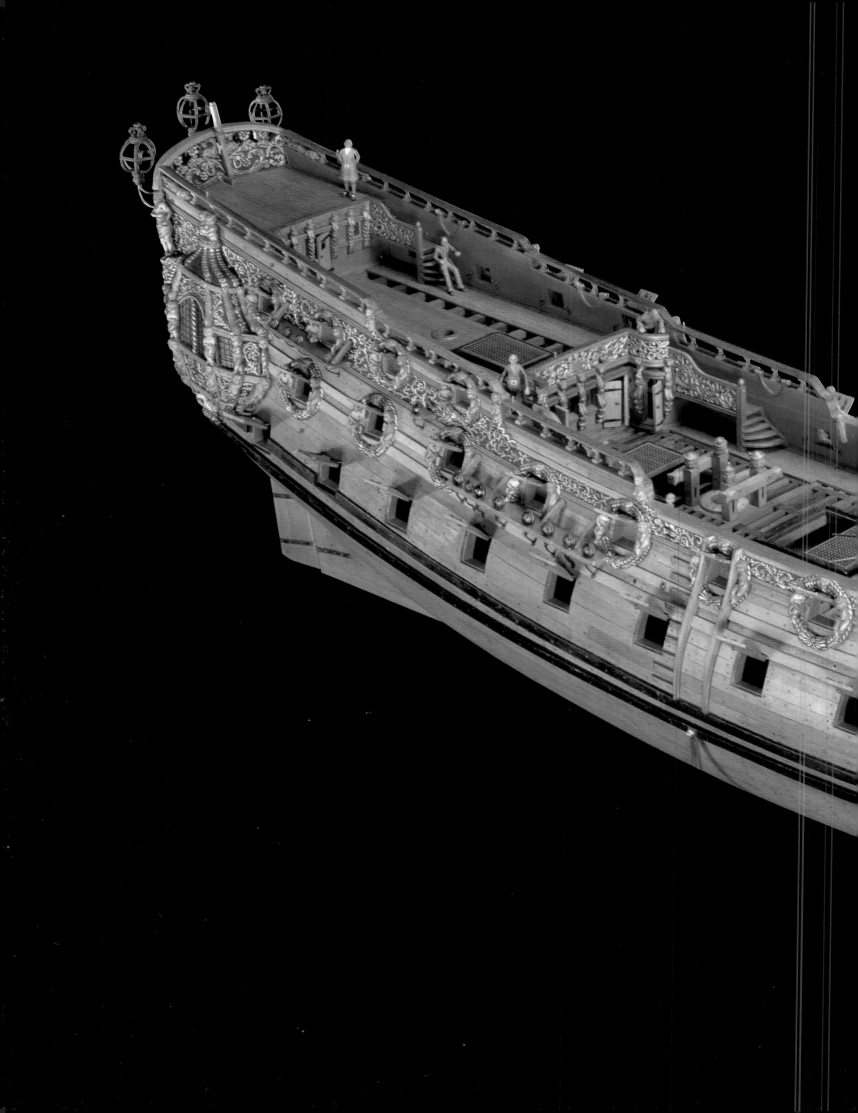

The seventeenth century was the golden age of ship carving and gilding, with every shipyard seemingly employing as many artists and sculptors as plankers and caulkers. The English built a series of riotously decorated ships, culminating in 1637 with the *Sovereign of the Seas*, one of the largest sailing ships constructed to that date and a monument to decorative excess. Among her hundreds of gilded ornamentations were an equestrian sculpture of King Edgar riding in victory over the bodies of his enemies, a cupid riding a lion, the likenesses of mythological gods and goddesses, biblical and allegorical figures, plus wreaths, fans, vines, and assorted curlicues. Of her construction cost of £65,586, a total of £6,691 went to the carvers and gilders.

Fifty years later, the fashion for decoration had abated somewhat, but no one could yet accuse the shipbuilders of restraint. This English fifty-gun ship, built in 1687, is embellished with more than 250 individual carvings of people, animals, and mythological characters.

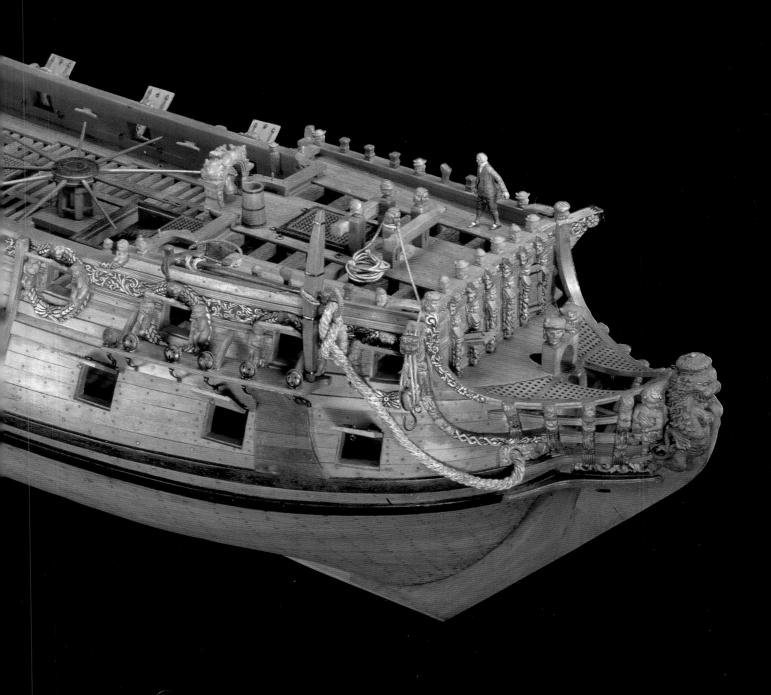

THE VASA
STORY

*It was just a small gust of wind,
a mere breeze,
that overturned the ship.*

— CAPTAIN SOFRING HANSSON
of the royal ship *Vasa*

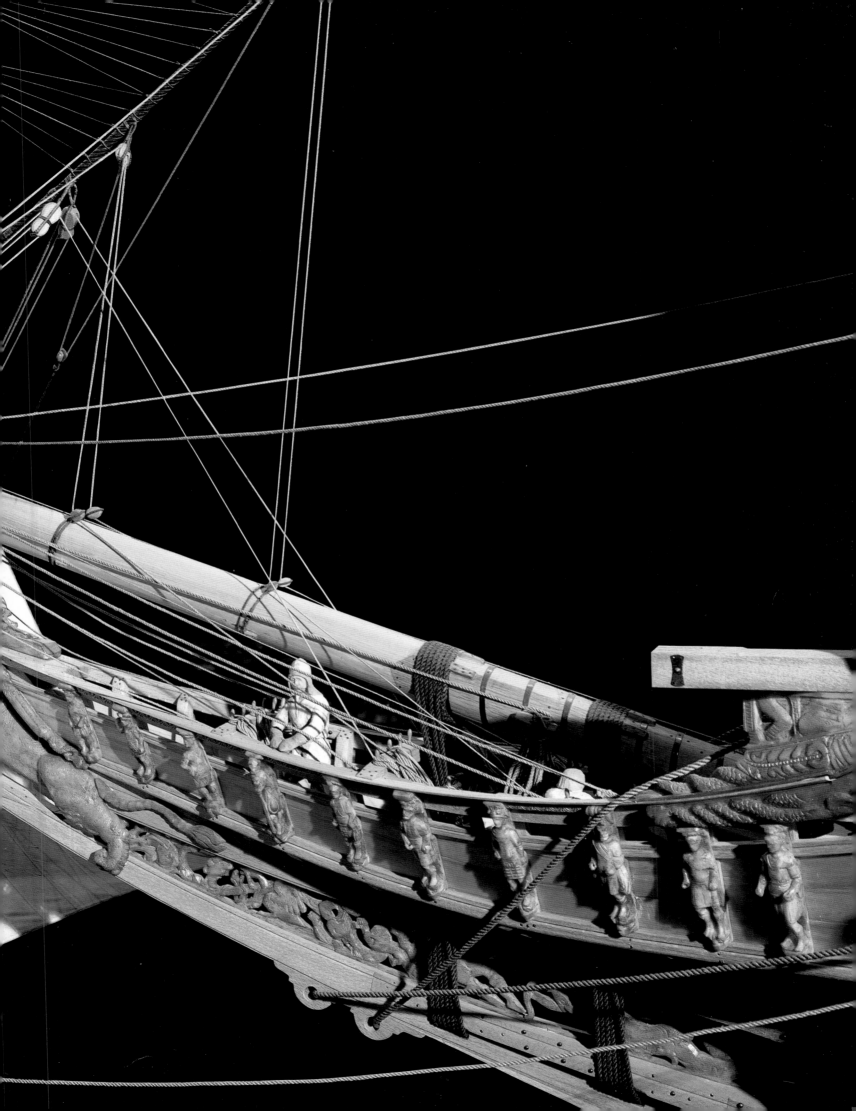

ON THE AFTERNOON OF AUGUST 10, 1628, the sixty-four-gun *Vasa*, at nearly 180 feet long the largest and mightiest ship of the Swedish Navy, set sail from Stockholm Harbor in a light breeze on her maiden voyage. A short distance from the dock, the crew opened the gunports, ran out the guns, and fired a celebratory salute. Less than a mile away, in full view of a huge crowd of well-wishers who had gathered along the shore to see her off, the ship was struck by a sudden gust. She heeled over onto her side, filled with water through her open gunports, and sank like a stone in more than a hundred feet of water. Of the several hundred people on board, approximately fifty were drowned. A brand-new ship — the grandest in the fleet and the hope of a nation locked in the Thirty Years' War — was irretrievably lost.

As in all tragedies, there was blame to be assigned — but to whom? The designer claimed that if the ship had been built properly and handled in a seamanlike manner, it would have survived the strongest winds, never mind a gust of short duration. The shipyard claimed that the plans of the ship, which had been approved by the king himself, had been followed to the letter. The captain claimed that he had been prudent in the handling of the ship — only a fraction of her very large inventory of sails had been set, and the heavy naval guns had been lashed down securely to prevent their sliding to one side and upsetting the stability of the hull.

More than three centuries would pass before naval architects were able to examine the evidence and render an opinion: The *Vasa* was extremely top-heavy. The shape of her hull and the ballast in the deepest part of her hold were not sufficient to counter the weight of her masts, spars, and rigging, and, most especially, the weight of her guns. If all of her sails had been set, the *Vasa* would have been knocked down by an even slighter breeze than the one that actually led to her sinking.

But one age's loss would become another's gain. If the *Vasa* had not sunk in Stockholm Harbor, if she had gone into battle and been destroyed, or had lived a long life and then been dismantled, we would never have known what she was really like.

For nearly fifty years after the sinking of the *Vasa*, several attempts were made to salvage the vessel. The masts of the ship were so tall that the tops, with pennants still flying, pierced the surface of the water, marking her location. French salvagers tried their hand, then the English, the Dutch, and the Germans. When raising the ship failed, attention turned to her guns; above all else, the king's armorers wanted those valuable weapons back. Finally, in 1664–65, using crude diving equipment, a team of Swedes and Germans managed to rip off the top deck of the ship

and remove about fifty of the cannons.

The raising of the *Vasa* herself, still lying upright on the bottom, was given up as a lost cause. Her masts cleared away so as not to restrict navigation in Stockholm Harbor, she was soon only a dim memory, one of those unfortunate losses in an era when hundreds of ships were wrecked or destroyed in combat in any given year. Her exact location was forgotten; she lay undisturbed for more than three centuries on the bottom of the harbor, a time capsule waiting to be opened.

In 1954, Anders Franzen, a Swedish maritime-history enthusiast, began an intense search for the location of the *Vasa*. Noting that the teredo, a marine worm responsible for the destruction of wood underwater, requires water with a salinity of .9 percent to survive, while the salinity of Stockholm Harbor was .7 percent, Franzen surmised that the *Vasa* might have remained intact. For the next two years, he swept the floor of the harbor with grapnels and wire drags and used a homemade core sampler to explore the bottom. All he could dredge up were old bedsprings, rubber tires, rusty stoves, and tin cans — until one momentous day in the summer of 1956 when his core sampler retrieved a piece of centuries-old blackened oak.

A few days later, a diver descended into the murky water and in short order swam into a wall of wood. It was the side of the *Vasa*.

The most complete seventeenth-century wooden ship ever discovered, the *Vasa* was immediately recognized as a Swedish national treasure. A decision was made to raise the vessel intact, preserve her carefully, and install her in a museum on the harborfront not far from where she was built.

The salvage method used involved boring tunnels under the hull, passing steel cables through, and then lifting her bodily with winches attached to salvage pontoons on the surface. Divers worked underwater for more than two thousand hours to accomplish that and more. When they were done, on April 24, 1961, the *Vasa* broke the surface and was towed to a drydock for conservation and preservation. By the time the archaeologists had finished exploring her, they had found thousands of objects — from ship's tools and gear to clothes and personal possessions, art objects to candlesticks and lamps. Best of all, they had in drydock a huge wooden ship, 95 percent intact, exactly as she had been when built.

Using the same preservation techniques later adopted by the Danes for the Viking ships raised at Roskilde, the Swedish conservators installed the *Vasa* in a sealed room, where she was sprayed with a solution of polyethylene glycol and water, twenty-four hours a day, for several years. Finally, in December 1988, she was moved across the harbor to the specially constructed Vasa Museum, where she is now on permanent display. To ensure the *Vasa*'s preservation, the environment in the room where she is kept is maintained at a constant humidity of 60 percent and temperature of 20°C — with strict limitations on the amount of light.

A capital ship — that is, one of the principal vessels of the battle fleet — the *Vasa* is impressive in all respects. Shipyard records indicate that her construction required approximately a thousand oak trees. Her displacement is more than 1,200 tons, and she is approximately 180 feet long from stem to stern. She has two gun decks carrying sixty-four bronze cannons and accommodations for 145 seamen and 300 soldiers.

When the *Vasa* went down, she was rigged with three masts and ten sails, six of which were found in the wreck. A product of the golden era of ship ornamentation, she was decorated with more than two hundred carved ornaments and five hundred sculptures — lions, devils, angels, musicians, warriors, cupids, Roman emperors, mythological characters, the coat of arms of the Swedish royal family, and more.

Take it all in all, a ship is the most honourable thing that man,
as a gregarious animal, has ever produced.

— JOHN RUSKIN

SHIPS OF WAR

The press of canvas she was carrying laid her over, until her copper sheathing, clear as glass, and glancing like gold, was seen high above the water, throughout her whole length, above which her glossy jet black bends, surmounted by a milk-white streak, broken at regular intervals into eleven goodly ports, from which the British cannon, ugly customers at best, were grinning.

— from *Tom Cringle's Log*, MICHAEL SCOTT

FOR ALL HER GRANDEUR, the royal ship *Vasa* was not designed to satisfy the creative impulses of her builders. Rather, she was intended to project sea power, the key to prosperity in an age when commerce was the major method of increasing national wealth. Warships were a form of investment; the more you had and the better they worked, the better able you would be to protect your merchant ships from the warships of your enemies. That the *Vasa* was encrusted with carvings and giltwork was a subtle message to the competition: Sweden had been successful in the exercise of sea power — the proof of the resulting wealth was expressed in the opulence of her naval vessels — and the king, by ordering more expensive ships, was

expressing his confidence that such success would continue.

Britain, France, Holland, and Spain needed immense sums of money to build and maintain their grand naval fleets, yet they were seen as worth the investment, because they protected the unarmed — or lesser armed — ships that brought home the wealth that could raise the standard of living and pay for the navy in the first place. Great merchant nations that suffered major naval defeats, as Spain and Holland did at the hands of the British, simply ceased to be great merchant nations.

None of this was lost on the national policymakers of the eighteenth and nineteenth centuries. Monopolies and trade routes had to be protected, or else they would be lost to the competition. The naval establishments of the great European powers were therefore of primary concern, with shipyards and dockyards distributed along the coasts for the express purpose of building and maintaining the fleets. The countries with the best designers and shipwrights, and the infrastructure to support them — the timber plantations, the ropewalks, the shipsmiths, the gunmakers, the sailors — achieved primacy. Those that did not, failed.

In the eighteenth century, the ships of the English navy, and some of the other European navies as well, were divided into six rates, or classes, which defined their power and relative importance. Those of the first rate were considerably larger, more powerful, and heavily manned than those of the second down to the sixth. The third-raters, particularly the seventy-four-gun ships, were the workhorses of the fleet. At the end of the eighteenth century, for example, the French and the English navies — the most powerful of the time — had more seventy-fours than any other type of ship.

Built in 1760, the *Bellona* was a typical seventy-four of the time, measuring 168 feet along her gun deck and weighing a little more than 1,600 tons. She served in many of the great campaigns when the French and the English fought for European supremacy. Here she is on the ways at the Portsmouth Dockyard, where she was refitted and given a copper-clad bottom in the period between 1778 and 1782.

After much experimentation over the centuries, the English navy at the end of the eighteenth century turned to coppering the bottoms of their ships as protection against teredos (shipworms) and marine growth. The copper was applied in thin plates and fastened with copper nails, and as long as it remained intact, the metal provided an impenetrable barrier against worms trying to attack the wooden planking. What's more, it interacted with salt water to produce a slightly poisonous solution that kept sea weeds and grasses from growing on the hull. (A ship fouled with weed was slower than one with a clean surface.)

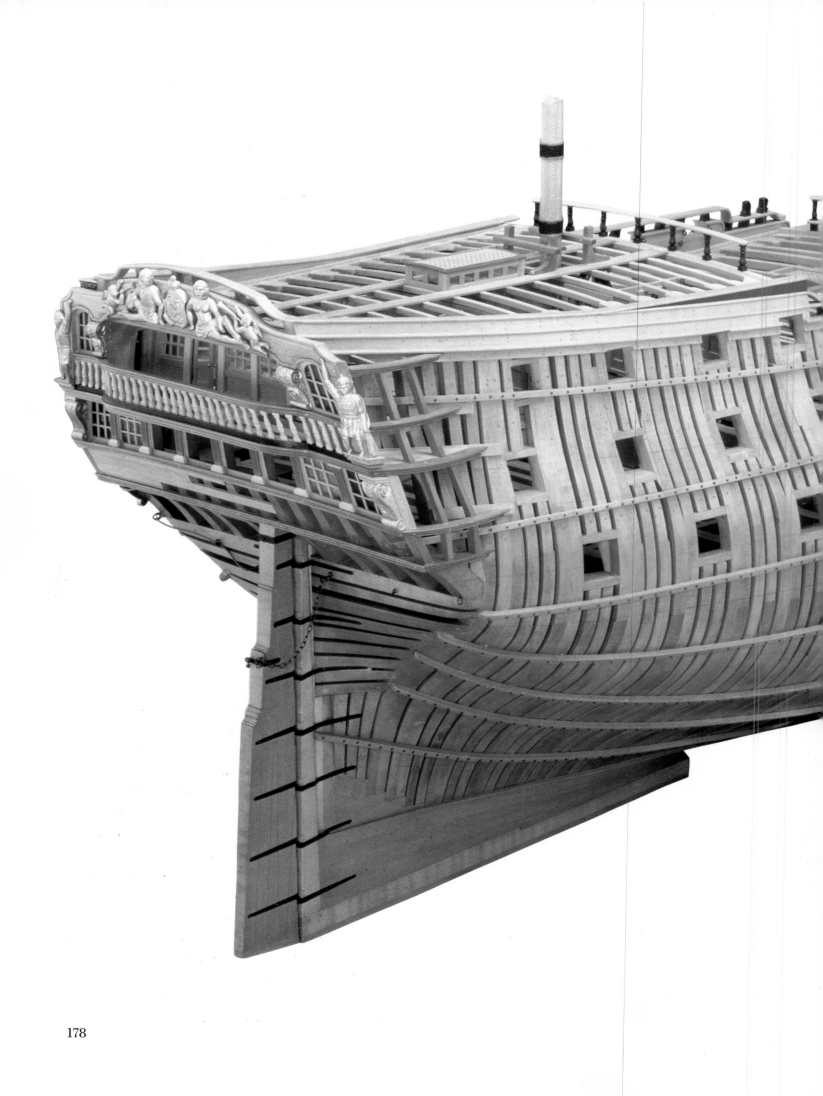

Wooden ships-of-the-line — major battleships — required massive amounts of timber and materials in their construction. A third-rater like this would need roughly 2,000 trees, 100 tons of ironwork, 4,000 sheets of copper, 30 tons of copper bolts, 30,000 trunnels, 12 tons of oakum, 5 tons of pitch, 12 tons of tar, 6 tons of whiting and white lead, and more than 4 tons of paint.

English shipbuilders preferred English oak for their ships, believing that species to be stronger and longer lasting than continental and American oaks; the latter, in fact, were thought to be more prone to rot, although American shipbuilders have used native white oak to great advantage for centuries.

Ensuring an adequate supply of oak for shipbuilding was a nagging problem for the English naval establishment. As the wars, especially with the French, came more frequently, and the warships became larger and more numerous, the shipyards used oak faster than it could be grown. Thousands of tons of timber were used every year — straight timbers for keels and planking, and compass timbers, crooked wood, for frames and knees — yet an oak tree took a century to grow to maturity from the time it was first planted. The government established a far-reaching tree-planting program, but by the end of the eighteenth century, it was not enough. Nonnative timber — second-rate stuff, according to the shipwrights — had to be imported. Most came from the Baltic region, but some came from Italy and North America.

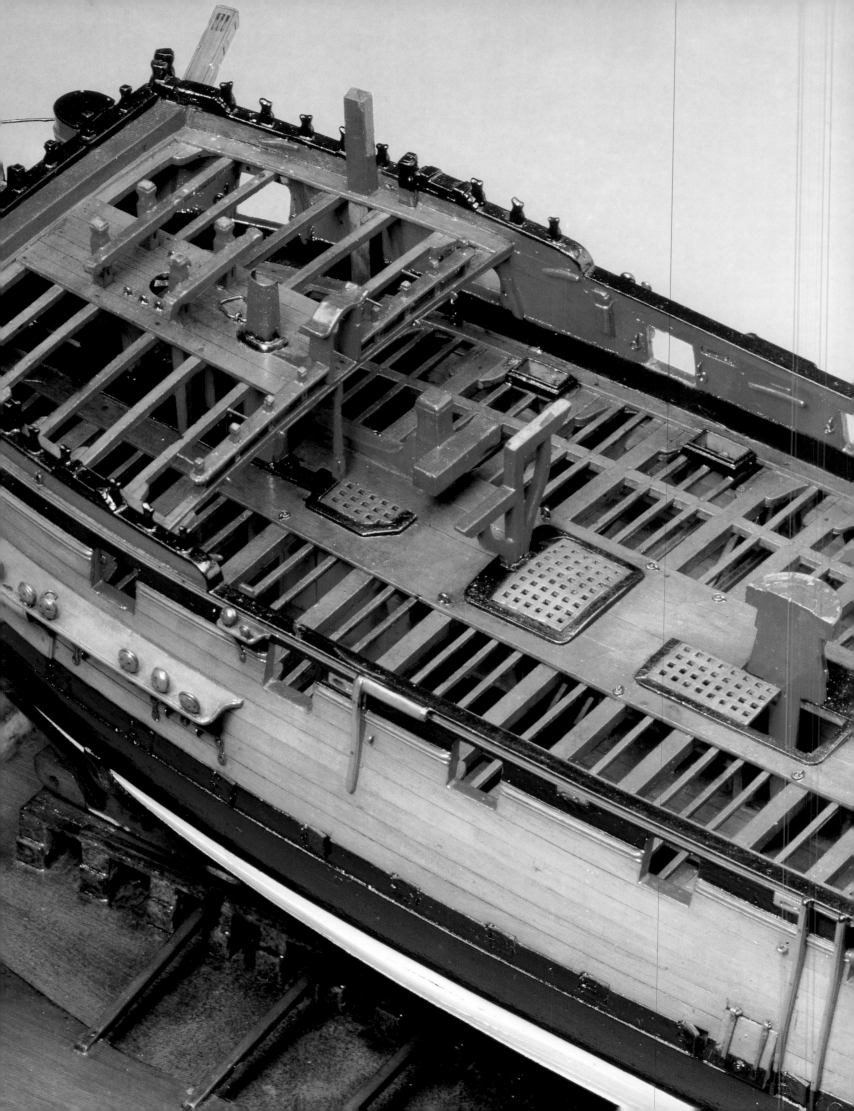

The deck structures of wooden fighting ships had to be
heavily reinforced and braced, much more so than in
merchant vessels, to carry the weight of the guns and
resist the strains on the hull when the guns were fired.
The deck framing also had to help the rest of the hull
structure resist the pounding of the enemy's cannon
fire. Using extra-heavy beams and carlins, however,
was not the answer, as large timbers would create too
much weight too high in the hull. Such a deficiency, in
company with the tremendous weight of the guns,
could raise the center of gravity, making the ship
"crank" — a tendency to roll too quickly in a
seaway — or, in the worst case, unstable.

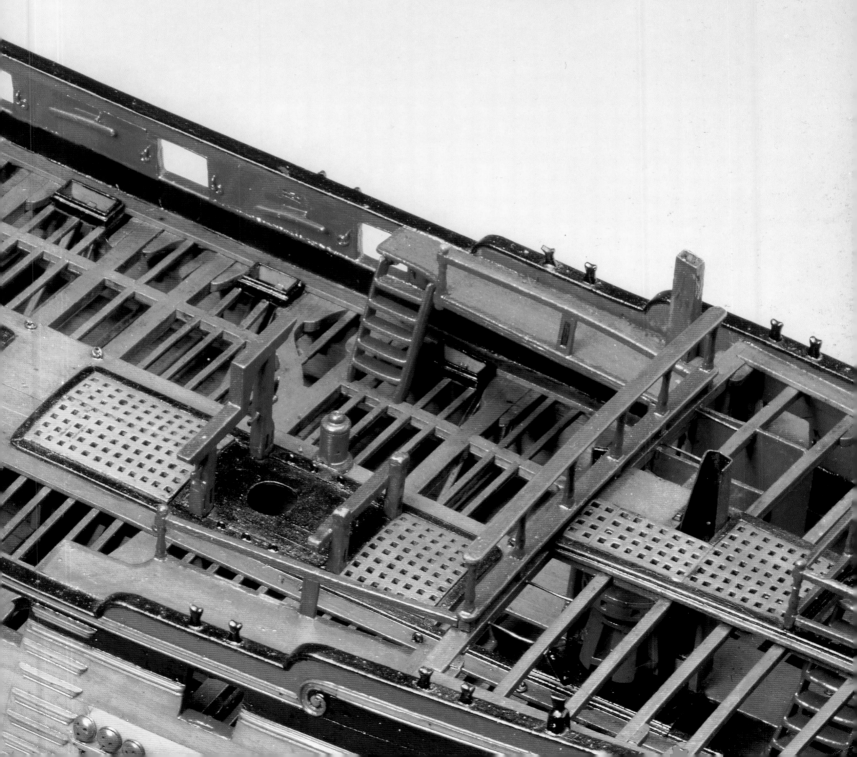

As the wooden fighting ships of the first rate became larger and more powerful — by the Napoleonic Wars, the largest ships carried 120 guns — the engineering of the hull structure became more complex. Given the dimensions of the timbers available, there was a limitation on the size of a wooden hull beyond which it could not stand the strains induced by its own weight and that of its guns, gear, and provisions. To overcome this problem, the shipbuilders added what were known as riders to the inside of the hull, directly over the ceiling, the layer of longitudinal planking inside the frames. Shortly after the beginning of the nineteenth century, this method was superseded by the use of diagonals and longitudinals to create a series of triangles over the ceiling. Known as the Seppings system — after its inventor, Sir Robert Seppings — it was the predecessor of the iron strapping used to reinforce the structure of wooden ships toward the end of the nineteenth century.

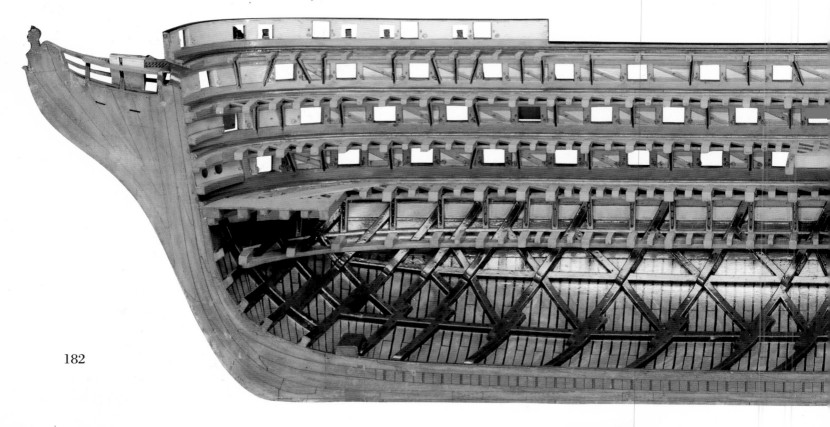

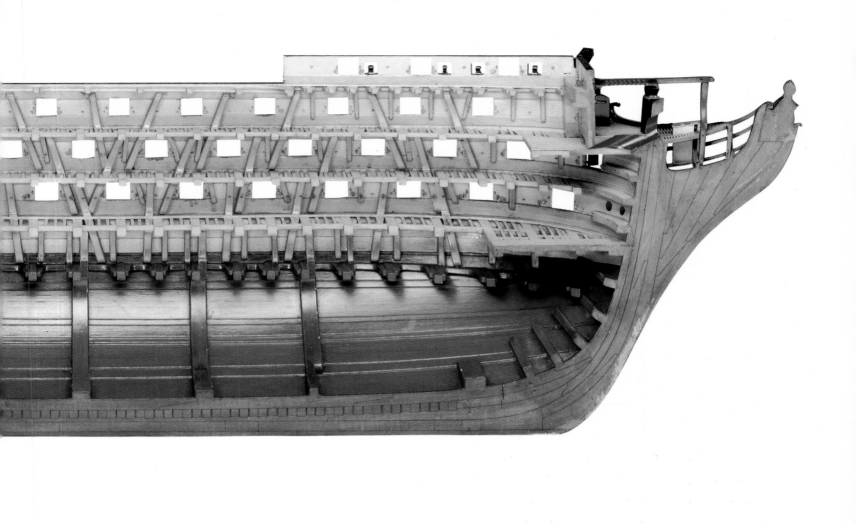

The two weakest parts of the hull of a wooden fighting ship were along the sides, where the planking and framing were interrupted by the gunports, and the overhanging stern, which was extremely difficult to support and therefore had to be lightly constructed. The problems caused by the gunports were solved by staggering them so that there would be enough space between gunports to allow at least one pair of frames to extend unbroken from keel to rail. The solution to the overhanging stern was to do away with the old-style square stern (left), which required several horizontal timbers to reinforce it and derived very little support from the sternpost and keel, and replace it with the round stern (right). The beautiful round stern, developed by Sir Robert Seppings, could be framed entirely with vertical timbers tied to the keel by way of the sternpost.

As in all navies in all eras, the major battleships, for all their concentrated power, constituted only a fraction of the fleet. Backing them up and providing assistance was a variety of smaller, specialized ships and boats. There were fast dispatch cutters and sloops, bomb ketches, fire ships, transports, and others.

This is the American brig *Lexington*, 90 feet long and armed with sixteen four-pound guns. Lightly constructed in comparison to the ships-of-the-line, she was a merchant vessel converted to a commerce raider and dispatch ship at the beginning of America's Revolutionary War. She was relatively fast and maneuverable, and a smart sailer.

185

The newly independent United States officially established a navy in 1794 in response to threats to American commerce from the Barbary pirates and the French. The Americans did not have the establishment or the resources to compete with the major European navies with their capital ships, so they concentrated on cruisers — more powerful than the frigates of the fifth and sixth rates, fast enough to outsail anything larger. Six nearly identical ships were built, among them the soon-to-be-legendary *Constitution*, 175 feet long and rated to carry forty-four guns. During the War of 1812, she won several battles against larger British ships and in the process gained her nickname, "Old Ironsides," in recognition of the strength of her construction.

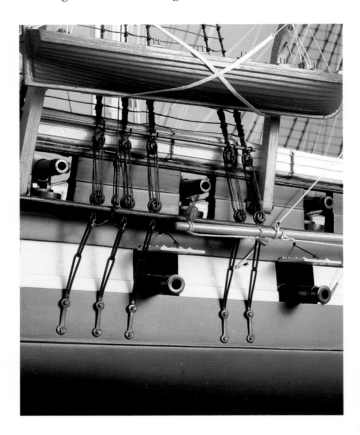

Several shots now entered our hull. One of the largest the enemy could command struck us, but the plank was so hard it fell out and sank in the waters. This was afterwards noticed and the cry arose: "Huzza! Her sides are made of iron! See where the shots fell out!"

— MOSES SMITH, sponger of gun no. 1 aboard the *Constitution* during her battle with the frigate *Guerrière*

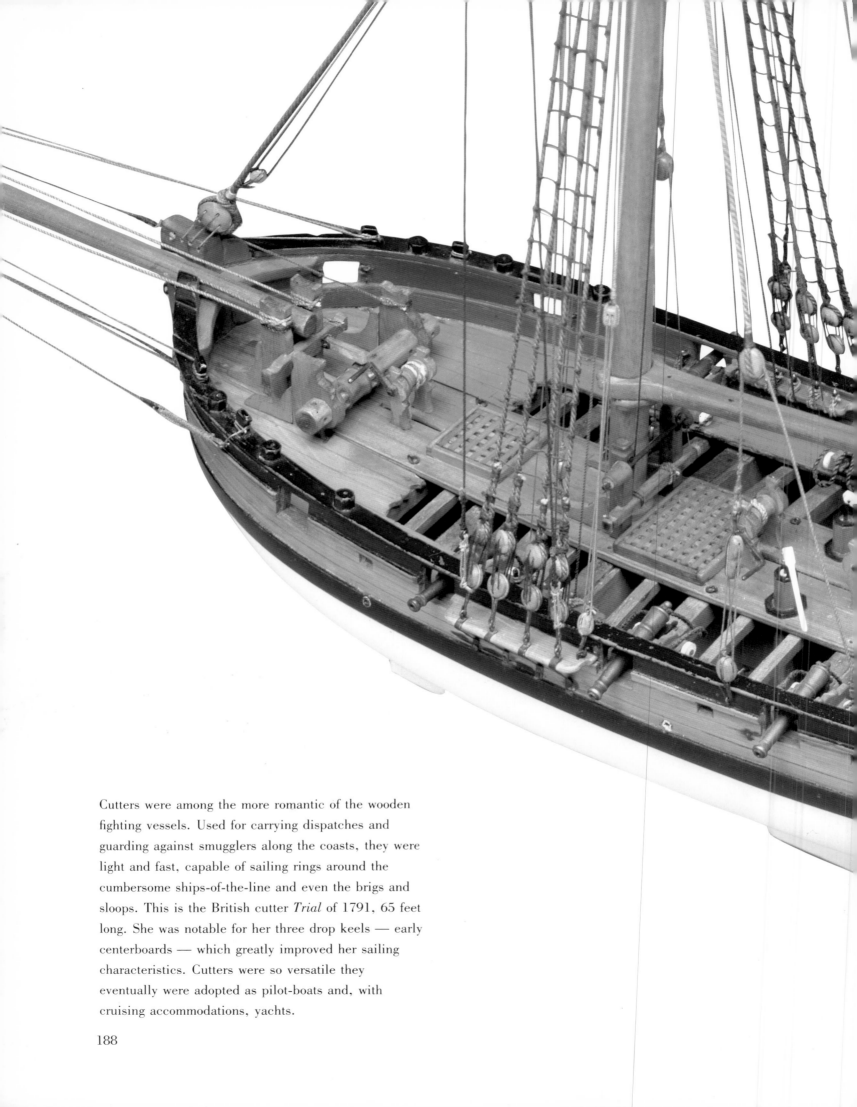

Cutters were among the more romantic of the wooden
fighting vessels. Used for carrying dispatches and
guarding against smugglers along the coasts, they were
light and fast, capable of sailing rings around the
cumbersome ships-of-the-line and even the brigs and
sloops. This is the British cutter *Trial* of 1791, 65 feet
long. She was notable for her three drop keels — early
centerboards — which greatly improved her sailing
characteristics. Cutters were so versatile they
eventually were adopted as pilot-boats and, with
cruising accommodations, yachts.

The smallest wooden naval craft were the ship's boats, which may seem insignificant, but in fact they were indispensable for communicating with the shore and other ships of the fleet, loading provisions and ammunition, exploring unfamiliar coastlines, carrying anchors, and even towing the ship under oars during a calm.

This thirty-six-gun frigate of 1805 carries three boats on her main deck. The usual practice, as here, was to lash the boats down to the spare topmasts and yards, which in turn were lashed to the deck. The two smaller boats are launches or pinnaces, primarily for transporting sailors from ship to shore. The larger of the three is the longboat, a strongly constructed craft used for carrying such heavy objects as anchors, guns, and water casks. Like most small boats carried aboard ship, it could be rowed or rigged for sail.

Despite the large numbers, only a tiny fraction of wooden ships and boats were built for war or defense. The vast majority were for fishing, ferrying, and especially trade — the seagoing import-export business of all but those countries so unfortunate as to lack access to the sea. How many wooden vessels would that be? Worldwide statistics have never been kept on the subject, but an appreciation for the number can be gained by considering that Holland alone in the mid-seventeenth century was estimated to possess about six thousand coastal trading vessels and fishing craft, and about a thousand oceangoing merchant ships. Britain, France, Spain, Portugal — much larger countries — had significantly more vessels.

Until recent years, there were hundreds of thousands of shipyards and boatshops in the Western world building wooden vessels for fishing, trade, and commerce. Major yards, employing hundreds at the peak of production, built the oceangoing ships; minor yards, with perhaps a handful of workers, produced the coasting vessels and inshore craft. The centers, of course, were where the shipowning companies were located and where the raw materials — timber, especially — were readily available. For this reason, the greatest Western shipbuilding countries were in Europe, the Baltic, and North America.

above

A small shipyard on the Baltic Sea. Typical of hundreds of shipbuilding and repair facilities, it is simply laid out, with a minimum of enclosed shops and a maximum of open space for handling large timbers. The ship on its side in front of the bulkhead has been hove down so the yard crew can work on its bottom.

194

Despite their defeat in three successive wars with England in the seventeenth century, the Dutch still managed to hold on to their colonies and trading stations in the Far East. The Dutch East India Company operated in much the same way as John Company, maintaining its colonial and mercantile interests with a fleet of specially built East Indiamen.

This replica of the *Amsterdam*, an East Indiaman of 1748, was built in Amsterdam, the Netherlands, on the lines of the original ship. It is 150 feet long, 42 feet beam, and was constructed using a combination of traditional methods and modern techniques. Unlike the *Susan Constant*, the *Amsterdam*'s frames were laminated — that is, thin strips of wood were clamped and glued together to the proper shape and thickness. The original East Indiamen were built of oak planking over oak frames and backbone, but the reproduction used iroko, a tropical hardwood, as it is in greater supply and more durable.

Generally speaking, Dutch ships — warships, East Indiamen, and other oceangoing vessels — were wider and shallower than their English counterparts. The ships of both nationalities sailed in the same ocean, but the coastal waters and harbors of the Netherlands are shallower than those of Britain. To return to their homeports, Dutch ships must be of shallow draft, and to compensate for this, they must be wider to achieve stability.

This is the *Britannia* of 1840, the first transatlantic passenger steamer of the famed Cunard Line. Transitional in design, she has the appearance of a sailing ship that has been only slightly modified for steam power.

As steamships evolved and the need for auxiliary sail declined, they took on a look of their own. Auxiliary sail or not, however, steamships were the vessels of the future; in just a few decades, sailing ships were part of the past.

Because the early steamships required more coal for long voyages than they could carry, the first of the type were hybrids: half steam, half sail. In a pinch, when the coal ran out or to take advantage of favorable winds, the crew could raise the sails. The *Savannah*, for example, the first steam-powered vessel to cross the Atlantic (in 1819), actually steamed only a fraction of the time.

SHIPS OF WORK

SAIL DID NOT IMMEDIATELY give way to steam, but rather it gave ground gradually. In some areas, such as the transport of nonperishable bulk cargoes, sail continued to be economical well into the twentieth century. But steam, and later diesel, proved ideal for warships and passenger vessels. In North America, for example, mechanical power was only slightly ahead of commercial sail at the turn of the century, but afterward it gained ascendancy quickly. By 1907, it amounted to 60 percent of the total; by the outbreak of World War II, it was virtually universal.

Though the wind is free, sail in the modern era is a marginally economical power source at best, as the sailing vessel cannot depend on the winds and therefore cannot meet the rigid schedules demanded by industrial societies. Even steam, which made the first major inroads on the age of sail, has declined to a mere shadow of what it was fifty and a hundred years ago. We live in the era of the motor vessel — ships and boats powered by internal-combustion engines.

Working sail still survives, however, in a few less-developed regions of the world — isolated pockets of India, Bangladesh, Indonesia, the Nile delta, stretches of the Chilean coast — places where time is less important than cheap transportation. It also survives, to a very limited extent, on some parts of the Chesapeake Bay, where for years conservation laws have encouraged the use of sailing vessels for oyster dredging. But it is an artificially induced survival, not a realistically economical one. Without the conservation laws, sailing oyster dredgers would have been pushed out of business a long time ago by mechanically powered fishing boats.

No longer viable for their intended purpose, many of the former sailing cargo carriers and fishing vessels remain, although in different guises. Beautiful traditional ships and boats, the epitome of functionality, have been restored to original condition and preserved as museum exhibits. Others have been converted to pleasure craft, houseboats, harborfront offices, passenger charter vessels, everything imaginable. Some are little changed from their working days; others have been modified to such an extent as to be unrecognizable.

If there is one constant in the art of ship and boat design, it is that the function of the vessel and the region of its principal use will have a major effect on the shape of the hull. Deep-draft ships, for example — those with a significant portion of the hull underwater — are ideal for the open ocean and along coasts with deep harbors, but they are useless in shallow waterways, such as those found in the Netherlands. Dutch vessels, as a consequence, are typically wide, bluff-bowed, and shallow draft: the most efficient shape for the prevailing conditions.

Holland is one of the more watery regions of Europe, a country of what seem to be endless rivers, canals, creeks, tidal estuaries, and water impoundments, all part of a huge transportation system.

This small wooden boat, though now used as a yacht, is typical of the Dutch working craft of the past. It has the traditional rugged construction inherent in a vessel that would be as comfortable fishing in the inland seas as carrying cargo along the inland waterways. Easily handled by one or two people, its rig — a single mast with only two sails — is as uncomplicated as its purpose.

The water-roads are nothing less than canals intersecting the country in all directions. . . . Water-omnibuses, called *trekschuiten*, constantly ply up and down these roads for the conveyance of passengers; and water-drays, called *pakschuiten*, are used for carrying fuel and merchandise. Instead of green country lanes, green canals stretch from field to barn and from barn to garden; and the farms or polders, as they are termed, are merely great lakes pumped dry. Some of the busiest streets are water. . . . *The city boats, with their rounded sterns, guilded prows, and gaily painted sides, are unlike any others under the sun.*

— from *Hans Brinker*, MARY MAPES DODGE, 1865

Traditional Dutch watercraft have been likened to a wooden shoe, and this lovely canal boat does nothing to dispel that notion. A fine example of functional artistry, it was built by craftsmen with an eye for detail. The most mundane parts of the boat are treated with aesthetic respect: the white moldings along the sheerline, the black moldings around the cockpit, the understated decorations along the after edge of the cabintop. Even the crotch used to support the lowered mast has been given a graceful shape.

The masts of sailing vessels on the Dutch waterways are pivoted at the deck, so they can be lowered quickly for passing under bridges. Note the raised leeboards on the rails on each side of the boat. Leeboards are so named because only the board on the lee side of the boat, the downwind side, is lowered into the water. When the boat is tacked, or changes direction in relation to the wind, the leeboard that was down is raised, and the other one, the board on what has become the downwind side, is lowered.

Dutch watercraft are famous for their traditional carvings and understated use of color, though there always have been as many plain vessels as decorated ones. In the old days, the owners of the working canal boats lived permanently on board and therefore showed as much pride in their domiciles as they would if they had lived in houses ashore.

Decorating working boats with paintings and carvings has long been traditional in many parts of the world. The stem of this *moliceiro*, common to the lagoons on the Atlantic coast near Aveiro, Portugal, has been colorfully painted with, among other things, a traveling salesman on the window ledge of a hotel. Modern motif or not, *moliceiros* are of ancient origin. They are open sailing boats employed in the transportation of seaweed, which is raked in the salt marshes for agricultural use.

The sail of this former working boat is made of a modern synthetic material, but in keeping with the old-style looks of the vessel, the sailcloth has been dyed a traditional deep red. Before the introduction of synthetics, sails were made of cotton canvas, which would rot quickly in damp conditions unless treated with a preservative. To do this, the sailmaker soaked the canvas in a tanning solution made from tree bark, which had the added, unavoidable effect of red dye. The resulting color was known as tanbark red.

The rope, too, had to be treated with preservatives. Old-style rope, before synthetics, was made of such natural fibers as manila, hemp, and jute, which was coated with pine tar, also known as Stockholm tar, as a preservative. In its natural state, such rope was light brown in color; after tarring, it became deep, dark brown and, after long use, almost black.

One way or another, leeway — the tendency of a
sailboat to be pushed sideways in the water from the
force of the wind — must be overcome. Shallow-draft
craft employ leeboards and centerboards. Those used
in deep water — such as these French fishing boats
from the coast of Brittany — can achieve the same
effect with deep keels. Generally speaking, the deeper
the keel, the more effective the resistance to leeway.

right

There is a dark side to a deep keel, however. Along
coasts with large tidal ranges — deep water in the
harbors at high tide and extremely shallow water at low
tide, precisely the conditions in Brittany — there is
not enough water to float a boat, whether deep keel or
shallow draft. The tide goes out; the deep-keeled
vessels take to the ground and heel over on their sides.
This puts tremendous strains on the vessels' hulls,
requiring stouter construction than normally necessary.
To allow deep-draft vessels to stand upright on the
ground at low tide, the crews sometimes rig temporary
shores, or "legs."

Most newly built vessels are launched upright; that is, they are supported evenly on both sides and slide down the launching ways on their keels — a complicated method requiring the use of a cradle and shores. Stoutly built vessels designed to take to the ground at low tide, however, can handle the strains of a side launching, which doesn't require an elaborate cradle. This French *langoustier*, a lobsterfishing boat, is about to slide down the launching ways on the edge of her keel and the turn of her bilge, the area of the hull between the bottom and the sides.

right

Besides being effective against leeway, a deep-draft vessel can also handle a large press of sail. Such a hull, sometimes assisted further by heavy ballast, has a low center of gravity, which counterbalances the force of the wind in the sails. The sail area of this French *bisquine de cancale*, an oyster dredger, provides speed to get her out to the fishing grounds and power to pull her heavy dredges along the bottom. (Some shallow-draft sailing vessels can also handle large sail areas, but they must be wide in relation to their length or else carry movable ballast that can be shifted to the windward, or upwind, side of the hull to counteract the force of the wind.)

e hulls
the
a deep
be
many
this, it

In
nd
, the

ing rig
in
han
uch the
s set on

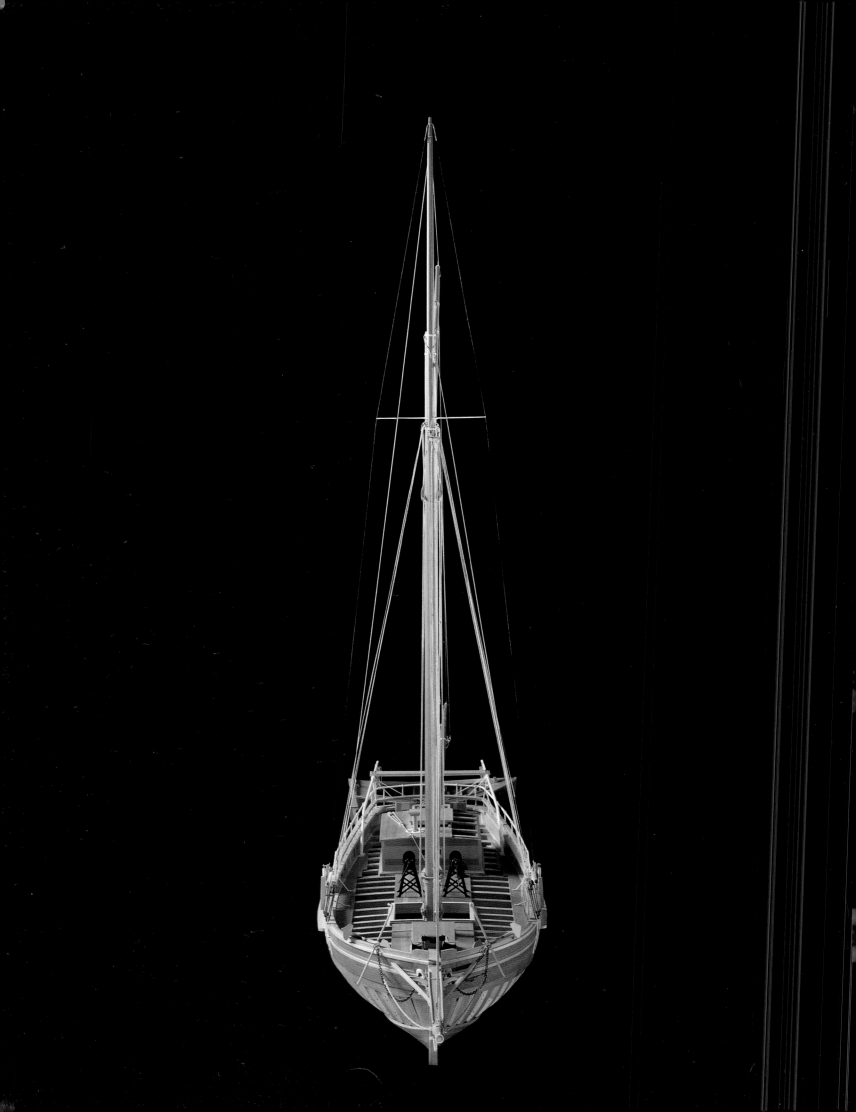

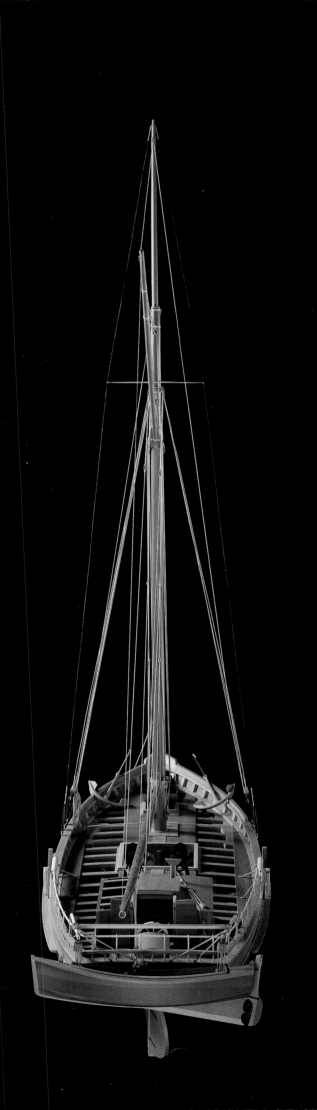

The small boat hanging from davits over the stern of this oyster sloop is a powered yawlboat. The oyster dredgers were built without auxiliary engines; indeed, most were built before the introduction of the internal-combustion engine. But in later years, during a calm or when maneuvering in tight quarters, the oyster dredgers were pushed by their yawlboats, which were fitted with large gasoline engines. The bow of the yawlboat fit in a notch in the stern of the oyster dredger. Other types of sailing workboats used the same method — notably the coasting schooners that carried cargo on the eastern seaboard right up to World War II. The skipjacks, which still dredge under sail for oysters on the Chesapeake, to this day carry powered yawlboats.

A Chesapeake skipjack, the *Rosie Parks*, a type of sailing workboat still used for dredging oysters on Chesapeake Bay.

213

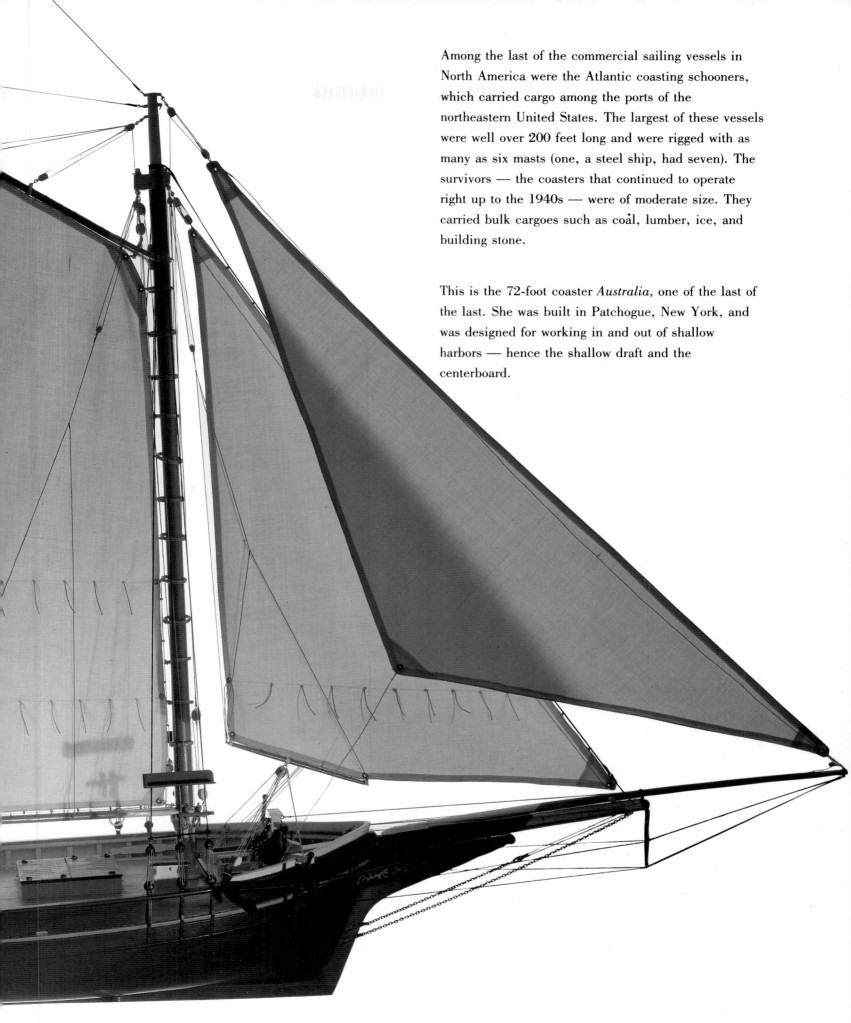

Among the last of the commercial sailing vessels in North America were the Atlantic coasting schooners, which carried cargo among the ports of the northeastern United States. The largest of these vessels were well over 200 feet long and were rigged with as many as six masts (one, a steel ship, had seven). The survivors — the coasters that continued to operate right up to the 1940s — were of moderate size. They carried bulk cargoes such as coal, lumber, ice, and building stone.

This is the 72-foot coaster *Australia*, one of the last of the last. She was built in Patchogue, New York, and was designed for working in and out of shallow harbors — hence the shallow draft and the centerboard.

SCHOONERS AND WHALERS

We trimmed 'er by th' wind an' I took th' wheel myself, an' we beat that vessel off er lee-shore, it blowin' er gale o' wind, with 'er deck full o' mack'rel, an' she never spilled five barrels of'n 'er deck, th' whole time we was er beatin' 'er off shore that day. She stood right up straight as er church-steeple th' whole time, walkin' right erlong an' she er sailin' fast, an' not mindin' 'er heavy deck-load o' fish 'tall. She handled like er play-boat, fer when I rolled 'er wheel down to tack 'er, she would comer erbout an' fill erway on tother tack nice as you please.

— CAPTAIN AL MASON of Gloucester,
describing his schooner, the *Carrie E. Phillips*

IN THE NINETEENTH and early twentieth centuries, a huge fleet of fishing schooners sailed out of New England ports, principally Gloucester, Massachusetts, but also Provincetown and New Bedford, and scores of harbors "down east," such as Portland, Boothbay, and Rockland in Maine. They fished far offshore on the Grand Bank off Newfoundland and Georges Bank off New England, and closer inshore on the productive grounds in the Gulf of Maine and around Cape Cod and the islands. There were so many fishing schooners at work that entire industries sprang up to service them. Every port with a fishing fleet boasted sailmakers, riggers, shipsmiths, coopers, ropemakers, netmakers, chandlers, ship designers, and, of course, boat and ship builders.

A schooner is a sailing vessel with two or more masts (the after mast as tall as or taller than the foremast) whose principal sails are of the fore-and-aft type — triangular or quadrilateral in shape — which is to say, they are not squaresails. Most fishing schooners carried two masts.

216

The schooner *L. A. Dunton* is one of the last survivors of New England's fishing-schooner fleet. Designed solely as a sailing vessel — many of her contemporaries were built with auxiliary engines — she is a living representative of a vessel type known round the world for speed, seaworthiness, and beauty. At the height of her career, she carried ten dories, which were launched from her deck every morning on the banks, good weather and bad, and from which her fishermen jigged for cod, haddock, and other groundfish. The *Dunton* was acquired in 1963 by the Mystic Seaport Museum in Connecticut, where she was restored and put on exhibit.

In America the principal kind of wood in wooden ships is and always has been oak, and oak is among the heaviest of woods. Since everything was done by hand, the work itself in the shipyards was, therefore, extremely heavy and hard. The timbers making up the backbone and frames of a ship were "beat out," as the expression went, with broadaxes and adzes. It took rugged constitutions and arms and backs of iron to do this and to stand it for ten hours a day, six days a week as they did for a great many years in the early decades of the nineteenth century. No wonder they stopped twice a day for a mug-up of good old New England rum. The cry "Grog-O" coming up in the middle of the forenoon and again in the afternoon must have been music to the ears of tired and sweating souls as they swung those great axes or struggled up a long brow or ramp under the crushing burden of a mighty oaken deck beam.

— DANA STORY, writing about the Essex shipyards

Essex, Massachusetts, partway up a tidal river a few miles from Gloucester, launched more wooden fishing schooners than any other town in America. Over 3,000 vessels are recorded as having been built in the town since records began to be kept in the late eighteenth century.

Essex built most of the fishing schooners that sailed out of Gloucester, including the great speedsters *Mayflower*, *Puritan*, *Columbia*, and *Gertrude L. Thebaud*. Almost all of the Essex schooners are gone now, but the *L. A. Dunton* is alive and well in Mystic, and then there is the *Adventure*.

Perhaps the *Gertrude L. Thebaud* was faster or the *Columbia* more beautiful, but the workhorse *Adventure*, built in 1926, is more symbolic of the skills of the Essex shipwrights and the traditions of the Gloucester fishermen. One of the last fishing schooners to slide down the ways in Essex, the last American dory schooner to fish the banks off New England, the greatest producer, the *Adventure* was built to work, not play.

218

Though modern for her time, the *L. A. Dunton* was a throwback in at least one respect — she was fitted with a bowsprit, the long spar projecting from her bow. To furl her sails, the crew had to crawl out on the bowsprit, a dangerous task in the foul weather and high seas common on the fishing grounds. By the turn of the century, so many men were lost at the bow that new fishing schooners, known as knockabouts, began to be built without bowsprits.

Unlike most working vessels, the American fishing schooners have a yachtlike appearance, as they were designed more for speed than carrying capacity. The first vessel into port from the fishing grounds obtained the best price for her catch, so swift schooners were much in demand. Some of the fastest banks fishing boats, in fact, were designed by yacht designers. The fastest of them all competed in the International Fishermen's Races between the Americans and the Nova Scotians.

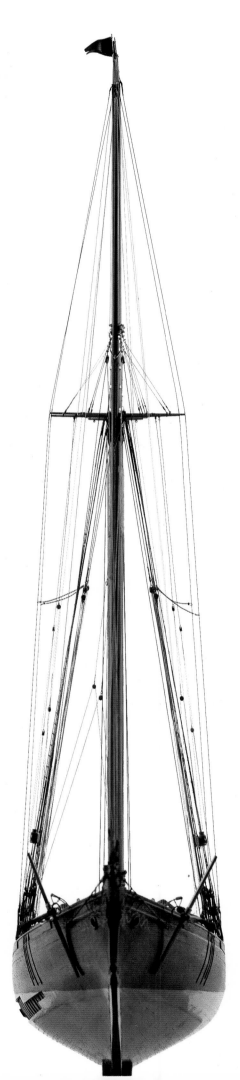

221

In 1954, the year after she retired from fishing, the *Adventure* was down in Rockland, Maine, taking passengers on weekly cruises along the coast. She remained in that trade until 1988, when her owner donated her to the citizens of Gloucester as a memorial to the once-grand fleet of banks fishing schooners that sailed out of that port.

Like all old wooden vessels, the *Adventure* has seen her share of decay. Yet like most wooden vessels that have worked for a living, she has stood up reasonably well to the ravages of the sea and of time because someone was always aboard to take care of her. Neglect kills wooden vessels. The *Adventure*, to her good fortune, has seldom been subject to much of it. But the time comes with all wooden ships that have been worked hard when, no matter the quality of the maintenance, she must be rebuilt. The frames rot, the stem becomes punky, the planking develops soft spots. In the worst cases, a substantial part of the vessel must be replaced. In the best, reconstruction is only required in isolated sections.

Space below decks on a fishing schooner was generous for the fish and limited for the fishermen. The purpose of the vessel, after all, was to catch and carry fish. Fish pens lined most of the schooner's hold. These were compartments where the gutted fish were packed in salt as a preservative if the vessel was on a long fishing voyage; in ice if she was making short trips for the fresh-fish market.

Fishing schooners like the *Dunton* and the *Adventure* carried a full complement of dories "nested" on deck — stacked one inside another — for their fishermen. One of the simplest and most versatile of small craft, the dory has been adapted over the years for groundfishing on the Grand Bank, inshore fishing off the coast, driving timber down inland rivers to sawmills, and a variety of other tasks along the working waterfront. The traditional dory is built of wide pine boards and is propelled by oars and, occasionally, auxiliary sail. The seats are removable to permit nesting.

These photographs of the *L. A. Dunton*, currently a museum ship, are deceptive. Although they show the layout of the schooner and much of her living accommodations, they were taken long after the crew had departed. The relatively tiny galley and forecastle on a working fishing schooner at sea would be filled with mattresses, blankets, drying clothes, seaboots, provisions, books, and everything else required on a long voyage. The hold would contain — besides the fish pens — shovels, rope, fishing gear, kegs and barrels, pitchforks, and the rest of the gear necessary to a working fishing boat.

The fishermen's quarters were Spartan and cramped, though not without the cozy warmth provided by wood and coal stoves in the galley and the main cabin.

Aboard most fishing schooners, the skipper and the mate berthed aft in the main cabin; the cook and the crew forward in the forecastle (pronounced foke-s'l). The bunks were built in tiers into the side of the hull, with limited storage for the fishermen's duffel under.

226

There was no privacy. The head — the toilet — was either a cedar bucket below or a seat in the open air up in the bow. The galley was a simple compartment, with a cookstove fitted with rails to prevent pots and pans from sliding off in rough weather, a counter, a few shelves and storage cabinets, and not much else. The crew ate, drank, argued, wrote letters home, and dozed at the triangular table between the bunks in the forecastle.

She was a ship of the old school, rather small if anything; with an old-fashioned claw-footed look about her. Long seasoned and weather-stained in the typhoons and calms of all four oceans, her old hull's complexion was darkened like a French grenadier's, who has alike fought in Egypt and Siberia. Her venerable bows looked bearded. Her masts — cut somewhere on the coast of Japan, where her original ones were lost overboard in a gale — her masts stood stiffly up like the spines of the three old kings of Cologne. Her ancient decks were worn and wrinkled, like the pilgrim-worshipped flag-stone in Canterbury Cathedral where Becket bled.

— from *Moby-Dick, or the Whale*,
HERMAN MELVILLE

Before the age of petroleum, one of the main sources of light lubricating oil, lamp oil, candle wax, and similar products was the whale, the largest mammal in the sea. But oil wasn't the only product of the whale; the bone and teeth were used for various manufactured and hand-carved items, including corset stays, knitting needles, and rolling pins. In the nineteenth century and into the first few years of the twentieth, hundreds of ships homeported in several northeast harbors of the United States — New Bedford, Nantucket, and Provincetown, Massachusetts; Long Island, New York; the Connecticut shore — roamed the oceans of the world on whaling voyages that lasted as long as three or four years.

Whaling was a rough, dirty trade, and the men who followed it were known for their independence, resourcefulness, and endurance. Yankee whalers were relentless in the pursuit of their quarry, for great fortunes could be made from a successful voyage. At the height of the trade, near the end of the nineteenth century, the whalers could be found in such far-off places as the South Pacific, the Indian Ocean, the Arctic, and the Antarctic. Their ruggedly built ships had to stand up to the ravages of the open ocean in all weather, as well as the ice of the polar seas.

Compared to other wooden ships of the time, Yankee whaling vessels were peculiar craft. Designed and built for endurance and carrying capacity, not speed, they were a combination of fishing vessel, floating slaughterhouse, warehouse, blacksmith and carpentry shop, and home away from home. They were bluff-bowed, heavily constructed, and piled high with the specialized tools of the trade — tryworks for rendering the whale blubber, boats for chasing the whales, cutting-in stages, chains, ropes, buoys, casks, barrels, and all manner of spare parts and gear required by a ship that remained on the open ocean for months at a time.

The *Charles W. Morgan* of New Bedford, Massachusetts, is the last of the Yankee whaleships. She was launched in 1841 and chased whales until she retired in 1921, making a record thirty-seven voyages that earned a total of $1,400,000 for her owners. After being laid up for several years, she was purchased by the Mystic Seaport Museum in Connecticut, where she was restored and is now on exhibit.

The most obvious mark of a whaleship was the number of small boats hanging in davits and lashed upside-down on deck. (The *Morgan* carried seven.) These whaleboats were lightly constructed double-enders used to chase the whales once they had been sighted by the lookout stationed high in the ship's rigging. Given the dangers of the trade, whaleboats tended to have a short life, so many of the ships that voyaged to distant seas carried several knocked-down spares below deck; if needed, they could be rebuilt and put to work.

The average Yankee whaleboat, only about 28 to 30 feet long, carried a crew of six and a tremendous amount of gear: six oars and six paddles; 300 fathoms (1,800 feet) of whale line, two tubs for holding the whale line and a bucket for wetting it; a keg of fresh water; a bailer; a keg with lanterns, tobacco, and food; buoys and flags; an axe; a foghorn; knives; a bomb gun and lances; several harpoons and hand lances; spars, rigging, and sails; and more.

Comfort on a whaleship was relative. The accommodations were more spacious than those on a fishing schooner, but nevertheless cramped when one considers that the crew on some voyages had to occupy the same space for years at a time.

As on most sailing vessels, the *Morgan*'s crew lived in the forecastle, a compartment below deck in the bow of the ship, pierced by the foremast. The bunks, built into the side of the hull, were in two levels. There was limited storage space under the lower bunks, but most of the crew's personal gear was stowed in sea chests, which were handmade and decorated to suit the tastes of the owners. This photograph is of the interior of the *Morgan* as she appears as a museum ship. On a whaling voyage, the forecastle would not be so spare.

The *Morgan*'s day cabin was a peaceful oasis aboard a ship that was otherwise crowded and noisy, especially during those times when a captured whale was being rendered into oil. While the crew was cutting the blubber into chunks and throwing it into huge vats of boiling oil, and the cooper was making and heading casks, the captain could escape from it all and relax below in relative comfort. In keeping with Yankee understatement, the only decorations are the fine moldings of the woodwork and the scrollwork of the grille over the door; the only luxury is the upholstered couch.

Away from home and hearth for years at a time, many captains of whaleships took their wives along. The *Morgan*'s captain, concerned for the comfort of his wife, had the ship's carpenter mount their double bed on gimbals, allowing the bed to swing with the heel of the ship under sail and therefore remain level. The common sailors in the forecastle were not as fortunate. When the vessel was heeled, they had to wedge themselves into their bunks or risk being tumbled onto the deck.

ENGINE POWER

THE GRADUAL EVOLUTION from sail to mechanical power began in the early nineteenth century with the introduction of the steam engine. But the first steam engines were heavy and bulky — not to mention dangerous — and were confined for the most part to ships, not boats. Generally speaking, mechanical power was not used in smaller craft until the last decades of the nineteenth century, when lighter steam plants were developed and small gasoline and diesel engines were produced. Even so, many decades were to pass before most small working craft were fitted with mechanical propulsion.

The design requirements for hulls using engines are quite different from those powered by sail. The first installations, most of which were unsatisfactory, were accomplished simply by pulling the sailing rig out of a vessel and installing an engine and a propeller. As years passed, the shape of traditional-style working boats changed in response to the new power source. Experience with conversions from sail to power convinced designers and builders that the hulls would have to be modified in the future to take into account the weight and torque of the engine and the resulting strains on the hull, the driving power of the engine, and the reduction in space for the crew and cargo.

An old Scandinavian workboat, cut away in cross section for a museum display, demonstrates the difficulty of installing an engine in a small craft. Even though this is a small, single-cylinder engine of low horsepower, it takes up a great deal of space and, worse, would require the services of a contortionist to make necessary repairs at sea.

The structure of a wooden boat must be reinforced to handle even the smallest engine installations. Strong engine beds of heavy timbers — tied into the keel, floor timbers, and frames — must be fitted, and a shaft log (a timber bored lengthwise to take the propeller shaft) must be installed.

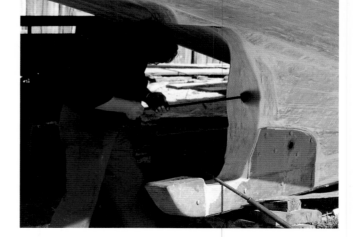

A fleet of small, open inshore fishing boats moored at low tide in the mouth of a tidal river in Staithes, a tiny port facing the North Sea on the northeast coast of England. The maze of lines keeps the boats positioned in the stream when the tide returns and the boats are afloat.

These are old-style boats modified for gasoline and diesel power. (The engines are hidden by engine boxes.) Their immediate ancestors looked much the same, but they were generally narrower, not as full-bodied, and powered by sail and oar. The bottoms of these boats are intentionally designed to take to the bottom at low tide without tipping over. The boat in the left foreground, the only one with a flat stern, is a coble, a type thought by some to have evolved from ancient Viking craft. The builders of these boats learned their trade from their fathers, who learned from their fathers, and so on, back into the unrecorded past.

As we progress further and further in time from the era of the sailing workboat, the engine-powered vessel looks less like a former sailboat and more like a vessel designed at the outset for mechanical propulsion. Despite that, the construction method — carvel planking over sawn frames, in the case of this Portuguese fishing boat — remains the same as the sea beyond the boatbuilder's yard. (The word *carvel*, for smooth-skin planking, is thought to have its origins in the fifteenth-century Iberian ships called caravels, which were planked in that manner.)

This Portuguese fishing boat from Nazare is designed and built to work in all weather off a coast noted for its high seas driven by storms off the Atlantic Ocean. Wide and flat at the stern to use the power of the engine most efficiently, it has a high, flaring bow and sharply raked stem to allow the hull to push into the sea and throw the spray to the sides. In the worst winter weather, when the seas are too great even for this ruggedly constructed craft, the fishermen of Nazare pull their boats far up the shore — some even into the streets of the town — to protect them from the winter surf.

ME 9608 H

Before the arrival of the internal-combustion engine, the lobster fishermen of Maine tended their traps in peapods — double-ended rowing boats — and sailing sloops. The lobstermen were limited in the territory they could cover and in the number of traps they could set. The gasoline engine changed all that, providing increased range and allowing larger boats with greater trap-carrying capacity.

The first power lobsterboats were the old rowing and sailing craft with an engine installed as an afterthought. Soon enough, the lobstermen discovered the inadequacies of such rigs and were collaborating with the builders on a design that would use power to the best advantage. The result, after considerable experimentation and evolution, was a distinctive lobsterboat that has much in common with the Portuguese fishing boat shown on previous pages — flat bottom aft; flat transom; sharp, raking stem; and a high bow. The principal difference, however, is that the Maine lobsterboat is framed with steam-bent timbers; the Portuguese fishing boat has timbers sawn to shape from crooked wood.

The first of the new powered lobsterboats were open craft with a box covering the engine, but most lobsterboats today have a cabinhouse with a wide windshield. Although all Maine lobsterboats look alike to an outsider, there are subtle but important differences among the boats of the various builders, each with its own supporters among the fishermen.

Wooden boat building gets into a man's blood. Alvin
Beal of Beal's Island, Maine, retired from full-scale
boatbuilding and immediately embarked on a new
career in model building. The Beal's Island–style
lobsterboat, evolved in the various shops of the Beal
clan, is famous along the Maine coast for its practical
perfection and honest good looks.

*When I was just a child my father used to take me over
to the yard and watch me. He'd put me in the shavings
and I'd play there while he was working. During my
school years I'd spend all my free time in the boatshop.
I'd go down there and sweep the floors and pick up
screws. I used to cut bungs [plugs] for the planking
gang. When they were building a small rowboat, I used
to crawl inside because I was so small, and I'd back up
the rivets for the plankers. I was seven, eight, nine, ten
years old.*

      — SONNY HODGDON, Maine boatbuilder

RECREATIONAL
SAILING

Ideas of Paradise are exceedingly various. To the ancients
Paradise meant a dolce far niente *in the Elysian Fields; to the*
North American Indians it means happy hunting ground and
plenty of fat buffalo. The Scythians believed in a Paradise of
immortal drunkenness and drinking blood out of the skulls of their
enemies. . . . To some, I believe, Paradise means yachting, and
for my own part, I think a 200-ton schooner, a ten-knot breeze,
and a summer sea hard to beat.

— SIR EDWARD SULLIVAN, 1894

Working sail — commercial vessels powered by the wind — may
be virtually a thing of the past, but there are still very many
wooden sailing ships and boats plying the bays, sounds, and
oceans of the world. The future of sail lies with the recreational
vessels — the former cargo carriers and fishing boats that have
been converted to pleasure use, and the yachts that were
designed and built for pleasure sailing in the first place. (The
most interesting of the latter, the traditional vessels, are actually
variations on old commercial designs.) There is, after all, an
elegance to vessels fitted out in an authentic manner, an
impression of solidity — one with the sea — that puts the
traditional wooden ship propelled by canvas spread on wooden
spars in a class by itself.

In recent years, several reproductions of old-style wooden sailing ships have been built. Some are museum vessels, intended for dockside exhibition. Others are for sail training. Still others are for promotional purposes, vehicles for "showing the flag." One of the most beautiful of these is the *Pride of Baltimore II*, the second vessel to act as a roving ambassador for the city of Baltimore, Maryland. (The first *Pride*, built in 1977, sank in a squall in 1986.)

The *Pride of Baltimore* is a Baltimore clipper, a type of ship that came into prominence during the period between the Revolutionary War and the War of 1812. Faster than any other sailing vessels of their size at the time, the Baltimore clippers were the favorites of privateers, pirates, and slavers. Rakish quicksteppers, they were long, lightly constructed, delicately sparred vessels, schooner-rigged with square topsails on the foremast.

The *Pride of Baltimore II* has the appearance of a historical Baltimore clipper, but, as a product of the modern age, she has the conveniences of our times — an inboard auxiliary engine, the pleasures of plumbing, long-lasting synthetic rigging, and more. The name *Chasseur* on the small boat carried in chocks on deck is a reference to the original clipper on which the *Pride*'s design was based.

In the rakishness department, at the opposite end of the spectrum from the *Pride of Baltimore* is the scow schooner *Vintage*, a blunt-bowed, shallow-draft workhorse that doesn't so much cut through the water as push its way over it. Think of her as a scaled-up flatiron skiff, modified with a V-shaped bottom, her bow sawed off and covered over with a flat bulkhead. The *Vintage*'s design is based on that of the old sailing scows that once carried cargo in and out of creeks, rivers, and coves where large, deeper-draft vessels couldn't go. Most of the space aboard such scows was given over to the cargo — hay, grain, coal, lumber, firewood — with only a corner reserved for the skipper and his deckhand. The *Vintage* is fitted out for pleasure cruising along the New England coast, not cargo carrying, so all of the space below is devoted to the comfort of the crew.

The color scheme here is typical of traditional working boats of the New England coast: buff decks and cabinhouse tops; white rails, spars, and cabinhouse sides; and dark green hull with a gold cove stripe. The bottom is coated with antifouling paint to protect it from barnacles, sea grass, and wood-boring worms; copper in the paint gives it a distinctive rusty-red color.

This cruising schooner, the *Kaiulani*, has the appearance of an old-fashioned cargo-carrying coaster, but unlike the *Vintage*, whose construction is as traditional as her appearance, she was built by the most modern methods. With a finish as smooth as that of a fiberglass boat, her frameless hull was built of thin strips of edge-glued wood covered with a veneer of mahogany bonded with epoxy resin; her decks are two layers of plywood glued together and then covered with teak planks. The resulting monocoque structure combines the finest elements of wood with the strength and longevity of modern materials. Everything on this schooner is designed for convenience and ease of maintenance. The sails and rigging, for example, are of synthetics, although a couple of her sails have been dyed to simulate the traditional tanbark red.

The *Kaiulani* may have been inspired by the workaday coasting schooners of years past, but down below she is the epitome of fine interior design. Instead of cargo holds and cramped living space for her crew, she has staterooms and a main cabin painted with an off-white enamel for brightness; varnished hardwood decks, moldings, and furnishings; bronze-framed portlights or windows; brass pipe for the flue of the cast-iron woodstove; and understated upholstery. Contrast all this with the accommodations aboard a genuine coasting schooner from the age of cargo-carrying sail, as described by Frederick Sturgis Laurence: "The crew's quarters," he wrote, "was a black greasy looking apartment with wooden bunks and a stench that would knock you flat. I wondered how many human beings could be content to sleep there."

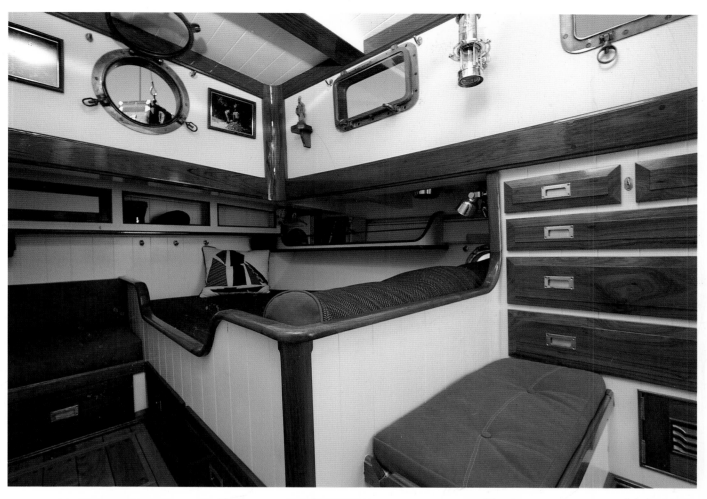

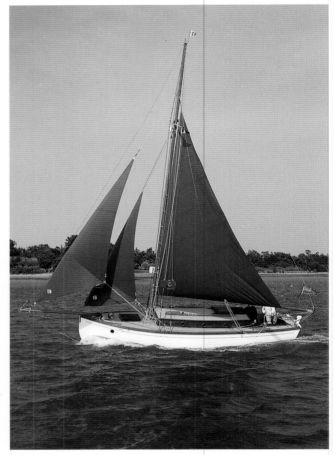

Some wooden boats, such as those once owned by Arthur Ransome, are better known in people's imaginations than they are in real life. Ransome was a British writer of children's books — *Swallows and Amazons*, *Peter Duck*, *The Picts and the Martyrs*, and more — almost all of which have a nautical theme. Many of the boats Ransome described in his fictional adventure stories were, in fact, based on real craft — some were his, some were owned by friends, some were recalled from his childhood. Thousands of wooden boat owners today are inspired by Ransome's enthusiasm for adventuring in small craft.

above

Nancy Blackett, a small cutter built in 1931, is very typical of the cruising boats then popular in the shallow waters of the east coast of England. A comfortable, unpretentious little craft, she isn't fast — but then again, she isn't meant to be.

right

"I am giving up my big ship on doctor's orders," Ransome wrote to a friend after World War II, "and am hoping to replace her by a much smaller, easier run vessel, a sort of marine bath-chair for my old age." *Peter Duck*, a cruising ketch laid out for comfort, not speed, was the result. She was so admired by other sailors that her design became the basis for an entire class of similar cruising boats.

left

Swallow is a 10-foot lapstrake dinghy, the second of that name owned by Arthur Ransome. He used the boat as a tender to a larger cruising boat and, being an enthusiast of open-boat sailing, as a sailboat in her own right. This little dinghy was built in the old style without plans or construction molds — entirely by eye.

Functional beauty is the hallmark of the well-appointed wooden yacht. Though the temptation is to varnish interiors to allow the grain of the wood to show, the result can be a dark, forbidding space, much like a cramped cave. The owner of the little *Freda*, a Victorian-style cruising yacht homeported in San Francisco Bay, chose to paint the interior with a warm cream enamel, highlighted by selected varnishwork. Hanging brass lamps, Spartan washbasin with a hand-pump faucet, folding table to conserve space, round bronze portlights, curved deckbeams to provide headroom in the middle of the cabin, simple yet comfortable bunks — this is a homey, unostentatious little wooden boat, a tribute to her owner and the craftsmen who built her.

One of the predecessors of the Maine power lobsterboat was the Friendship sloop, a "shippy" little craft with a long bowsprit, a small cabinhouse forward, and a large cockpit. It was named for the seacoast town in Maine where the type originated.

The original Friendship sloops, despite their salty bearing, were rather plain craft, with little varnishwork and minimal comforts for the crew. Long impressed by the seaworthiness of this sailing lobsterboat, yachtsmen adopted the craft after the fishermen switched over to powerboats. The yachtsmen polished them up and fixed them over with more comfortable accommodations. The resulting sloops — whether old ones made new or new ones with the appearance of the old — are charming, friendly craft that fit right in along the coast of Maine.

The Norwegian *redningskoites*, rescue ships, are vessels with such an illustrious past, plus a reputation for being the ultimate in seaworthiness, that they have been popular with cruising yachtsmen for almost a hundred years. Originally designed at the end of the nineteenth century to shepherd the Norwegian fishermen who worked the cold northern seas, these ruggedly built craft were noted for their ability to survive any weather, anywhere. When they were retired from the rescue service, many of the original *redningskoites* were converted to pleasure use; in addition, hundreds of the type have been built specifically as pleasure boats. Several have sailed around the world.

The 33-foot-long *Direction*, here punching her way through a sea, is a scaled-down *redningskoite* (the originals were about 15 feet longer). Rugged enough to survive shipwreck on the coast of Greenland in 1929, the first year of her life, she is still going strong today.

right

For hydrodynamic reasons, sailing vessels have less accommodation space than powerboats of comparable size. Restricted space on sailboats demands careful planning on the part of the designer and the builder. Interior joinerwork — cabinets, bunks, storage drawers, and the like — must perform their intended functions plus fit into the allotted space. On this cruising boat, high berths in the bow permit storage underneath but require a step for access; however, the step itself can be used for storage. Shelves for books and spare supplies can be provided atop the built-in cabinets, but rails must be constructed to keep everything from falling onto the bunk when the boat heels. Closed cabinets are fine, but in the damp environment of a boat at sea, they can encourage mildew; ventilation slots must be cut in the panels.

above

Details make the difference between a fine wooden sailing boat and a craft that doesn't quite measure up to standards. Though superficial looks have little to do with how a vessel performs, the design of the gear, its arrangement and maintenance, mean a great deal.

Consider brass chafing plates, intended to protect against wear in critical areas. Whether they are polished or not doesn't matter much, but if they are not placed correctly — if they are seen as mere decoration — they will not perform the function for which they were designed.

Wooden sailing boats — especially those of some of the well-known racing classes — are such prized possessions that some owners will go to any length to restore them to like-new condition and keep them that way. The racing sloop above, a former stalwart of the Alden Triangle class, is undergoing the throes of reconstruction, a process that no doubt will amount to as much work as if she were built new, from scratch. The boat below, a Dark Harbor 20, may be more than fifty years old, but she looks as if she just emerged from the builder's yard.

While modern boats seem to be a jungle of complexities — expensive winches, high-tech blocks, electronic black boxes, and whip antennas — those of the past, particularly pre–World War II, are notable for their simplicity. All that is required on a sailing craft, in fact, is not much more than a hull that will float her, a rudder to steer her, sails to drive her, rigging to handle the sails, and, if one wants to cruise for more than a day, minimal accommodations for health of body and mind. *Aida*, built in 1926, fits the description.

Aida is a New England boat — built in Rhode Island, maintained in Maine. Like all traditional craft from that region, she has a spareness to her, an austerity that is equivalent, in many ways, to a Quaker meetinghouse or a Congregational church without the religious trappings. These stylistic overtones go back to the earliest settlers of New England and were carried through commercial vessels as well as pleasure boats. Compare, for example, the day cabin of the whaler *Charles W. Morgan* (page 234), built in 1841, with the main cabin of *Aida*, built almost a century later.

Simplicity is not the dominant characteristic of many
sailing yachts. A yacht is, after all, an extravagance,
given over to play, not work. This is the 115-foot sloop
Astra, one of the most magnificent wooden yachts
sailing today. Actually, she is of composite
construction: To provide adequate strength for her
long, elegantly slim hull, her builders gave her a steel
skeleton — keel, frames, and deckbeams — and then
planked and decked her with wood.

MOTOR BOATS

THE POWERBOAT occupies its own niche in the world of wooden boats used for pleasure. Speed is the most notable element of that niche — engines, after all, are part of the equation — but there is more to it than that. It's the quality of the speed that matters. While a few of the wooden-powerboat enthusiasts, primarily the hydroplane racers, are interested in flat-out speed and not much more, most take a more subdued view: fewer screeching engines and shimmering roostertails of spray, and more stylish, comfortable, delicately refined speed — the type that makes one feel like the Prince of Wales driving his bride to Balmoral in a Rolls. That quality comes from the boat itself, not necessarily from forward motion through the water.

More than any other type of wooden watercraft, the antique and classic powerboat is in the grip of the collectors, the enthusiasts who buy, sell, trade, rebuild, restore, and refine the best of the motorboats produced since the era struck just before the turn of the century. Runabouts, commuters, Gold Cup raceboats — the more authentic, the better; the more varnished woodwork and polished brass, even better.

A Greavette power launch from Canada.

The first pleasure motorboats, other than old workboats retrofitted with an engine, were introduced at the end of the nineteenth century. They were basically steam-launch hulls with a small gasoline engine installed. Long, lean, open boats with oval cockpits, many carried fringed awnings to keep the sun off milady's head. They were designed for the protected waters of bays, rivers, and lakes, and were the perfect vehicle for enjoying quiet summer afternoons without a care in the world.

above

This motor launch, *Aida II*, built just after the turn of the century by Fay & Bowen, a major builder of motorboats, may have only a 10-horsepower motor, and she may not go very fast, but she is stylishly comfortable, one of the prime requisites of a classic powercraft.

The River Thames in England, especially the nontidal section between London and Oxford, has been a center of recreational boating for centuries. Noted for their beautiful rowing gigs and skiffs, the wooden boat builders of the Thames Valley turned their attention to motorboats and launches in the late Victorian and Edwardian eras, producing work of such quality that any of their remaining boats are prized by collectors. Thames wooden boats are distinguished by their immaculate detailing — careful matchings of woods and veneers, delicate striping, shadowed lettering, custom cast metalwork, and classically inspired proportions.

above right

Today several boatyards specialize in the restoration, maintenance, and even new construction of Thames River craft. The largest of these is Peter Freebody & Company of Hurley, a few miles downriver from Henley. The proprietor can trace his family's unbroken professional boatbuilding history back to 1809.

260

below The River Thames motor launch *Panther*, built in the
1930s and restored to like-new condition in the 1980s.

Commuting to work today is a hellish ordeal involving bumper-to-bumper traffic on the freeways and no parking when we get there, or tortured rides with the sweating mob in racketing subway cars. There was a time, however, when commuting was a pleasure. Back in the 1920s, 1930s, and 1940s, captains of industry and finance commuted by motorboat from their estates on Long Island Sound and upriver on the Hudson to New York City. Theirs weren't little launches and runabouts, either, but magnificent powerboats fitted

with all the comforts of home and club, and powerful engines to make the passage almost effortless. Motorboats used for commuting were known simply as commuters, and the largest of the type — virtually floating clubhouses — were operated by paid captains and crews. Many of these commuters still survive, and a few are even used for actual commuting. The vast majority are general-purpose yachts for harborside entertainment, coastal cruising, and chartering.

Motorboats are, after all, about speed, and while comfort has always been a desirable commodity in their design, there have always been those who thought that speed came first and foremost. The push for more and more speed dominated the early years of motorboating, just as it did automobiles, and certain designers and builders became famous for their successes. John Hacker of — not surprisingly — Detroit was one of the best of the pioneers, beginning his work just after the turn of the century. He designed a series of increasingly faster custom boats — several

record setters — and eventually established a company that built stock runabouts in the 1920s. An inveterate experimenter, Hacker created designs that almost always had their unusual aspects, but deep down they all were characterized by meticulous blending of wood and mechanical engineering, and a stylishness that was always ahead of its time. Antique motorboats designed and built by Hacker, or modern versions built to his designs, are among the most desirable craft afloat today.

Like almost all of the pioneer motorboat designers and builders, Christopher Columbus Smith, also from the environs of Detroit, began his career by trying to wring as much speed as possible out of the new motorboats. The faster your boats could go, the more notoriety, and future business, you would get. But while other designers and builders concentrated primarily on the custom market, Smith concerned himself with becoming the Henry Ford of speedboats. After a fling with speed for the sake of speed, Smith took his Chris-Craft company into the promotion and production of a runabout for every dock. By the 1920s, Chris-Craft was Everyman's speedboat. While somewhat lacking the elegance of the best of Hacker's work, the various Chris-Craft models — factory-built yet with high standards — became *the* boat to purchase off the showroom floor. That so many survive today, still driven as hard as they were when new, is a tribute to these beautiful craft and the staying power of well-engineered wood construction.

There was the screeching, screaming, piercing whine of an engine worked far beyond its legitimate tolerances; a line of flying spray passed before us. The noise stopped suddenly, and the spray fell in sheets to the water's surface. A long, sleek motorboat was revealed in the bright sunlight, rocking gently in the swell. Droplets of water slid down the boat's gleaming black sides, and a purple haze hung over it like an ethereal cloud. Sitting in the cockpit, staring straight ahead, was a stranger dressed from head to foot in a hooded jumpsuit of black leather.

— from *The Further Adventures of Expansion Man*, by
E.H. MORGAN

266

The greatest of the motorboats in the golden, early years of the sport were the competitors for the Gold Cup, a racing trophy as sought after as the Holy Grail. *El Legarto*, designed and built by John Hacker and powered by a modified Packard aircraft engine, won the cup in 1933, 1934, and 1935. A museum piece today, *El Legarto* lives on in her replica, *Happy Times*, a 70-mile-per-hour fixture on Lake George in upstate New York.

THE ART OF THE CRAFT

PANACHE, MAGNETISM, VERVE — *duende*, as the late commentator George Frazier used to say. At rest or underway, wooden boats and ships have all that and more, an indefinable style, an honesty, a perfection achieved only by the hands of artists and craftsmen.

Wooden ships and boats are not dead. The skills to build these vessels have not been lost; nor has the desire to sail them. Around the world, in the most unlikely places as well as the most obvious ones, this seemingly anachronistic type of vessel lives on, simply because the wooden ship, in all its incarnations, challenges the craftsman and quickens the heart of the sailor.

David Clarke, near Peterborough,
New Hampshire, uses spare time and recycled wood
to build his first cruising boat.

Ken Bassett's pulling boat.

Credits

The photographs are by Paul Rocheleau, except for those on the following pages:

A half-scale reproduction of the whaleship *Lagoda* under construction in the great hall of the New Bedford Whaling Museum. The original vessel, built in 1826, was 118 feet long. The reproduction, completed in 1916 and authentic in every detail, is 59 feet long.

Swallows and Amazons Forever